LOVE & BUSINESS by Erica S. Elliott

LOVE & Business

Book II.

Written By

Erica S. Elliott

ARNICA PRESS

LOVE & BUSINESS by Erica S. Elliott

Published by ARNICA PRESS

www.ArnicaPress.com

Copyright © 2019 Erica S. Elliott

Cover Art by Erica S. Elliott

www.EricaSwensonElliott.com

Printed in the United States of America.

ISBN: 978-1-7336446-3-1

This work is a memoir. It reflects the author's present recollections of her experiences over a period of years. Certain names, locations, and identifying characteristics have been changed, and certain individuals are composites. Dialogue and events have been recreated from memory and, in some cases, have been compressed to convey the substance of what was said or what occurred. This book is also designed to provide information, education and motivation to our readers. The author and publisher are not offering it as legal, accounting, or other professional services advice. The author and publisher make no representations or warranties of any kind and assume no liabilities of any kind with respect to the accuracy or completeness of the contents and specifically disclaim any implied warranties of merchantability or fitness of use for a particular purpose. Neither the author nor the publisher shall be held liable or responsible to any person or entity with respect to any loss or financial, commercial, incidental or consequential   damages caused, or alleged to have been caused, directly or indirectly, by the information contained herein. Every company is different and the advice and strategies contained herein may not be suitable for your situation. If legal advice   is required, the services of a competent professional person should be sought.

LOVE as BUSINESS by Erica S. Elliott

Book II.

How we sealed the deal

A true Story

Erica S. Elliott

ARNICA PRESS

LOVE & BUSINESS by Erica S. Elliott

~Illegitimus non Carborundum~

Don't let the bastards wear you down

LOVE & BUSINESS by Erica S. Elliott

TABLE OF CONTENTS

Nothing serves a leader better than a knack for narrative.
Stories anoint role models, impart values,
and show how to execute indescribably complex tasks.

Thomas A. Stewart
~Leaders on Leading: Insights from the Field~

Dearest Keith,

I found that description about the power of storytelling in your executive library. It happens to describe you to a tee. You achieved many complicated things in your wide ranging life. Your narrative, then ours have the virtue of being true. It is time for others to hear our stories, so they will survive when we are gone.

PICKING UP THE THREADS

~ *A meeting of the Minds* ~

When I left you in Love and Taxes, Book One, I was driving North on I-95 to the Philadelphia Airport to catch a flight to Atlanta, my new home. I was mulling over Keith's serious offer to get to know one another on a deeper level, a foray he launched over lunch at the Wilmington Club in Delaware.

After a few years of a phone and email working relationship, we now had met twice. And it was just as Roberta Flack sang, "First time ever I saw your face" it was a whole other level of connection. But before we physically met, the last thing on my mind was taking a big risk and starting over in a new relationship. And I certainly had no time for long distance liaisons or frivolous games, out of the question. I was what one of my friends dubbed a "serious girl."

But there was one chink in my emotional armor: a meeting of the minds. As you probably now surmised (if you read Book One) a big reason I loved my career so much was the cerebral engagement. It was an adrenaline rush every time that I solved an intellectual problem. But on a personal level, I didn't ever expect to find a man that was both mentally stimulating and interested in building a new life with me. But suddenly here I was, no longer alone in my thoughtful ivory tower. It was as if Keith catapulted like a cannon shot into the corridors of my mind. From there he found the secret door to the spiraling downward staircase into the middle of my heart. After recovering from my initial shock, I realized that I never wanted him to leave.

Besides being a tax client of mine, Keith had already finished a career as a powerhouse executive. For years, others regaled me with tales of his fearlessness on the business fields of battle, before we ever met. Now, coming face to face with the legend, I quickly nicknamed Keith Braveheart, after one of my favorite movie titles. The fact that he was also of Scottish descent, made it all the more applicable.

 In fact, Keith's offer sounded like he had pretty much made up his mind that he wanted me to join him in his newly retired life in Palm Beach. I could feel sincerity coming off him in waves of shimmering heat just like asphalt on a Southern summer's day. I believed that he truly meant it, but was it only for the moment? That was the question. What if the reality of living with a mid-career woman and her two elementary school-age daughters became a millstone around his neck?

I pictured raucous past moments of sisterly squabbles at the dinner table, where it seemed that I wore a virtual, perpetual referee's hat, as the single Mom I had recently become. Could these two very domestic lifestyles reconcile themselves?

Hannah, at eight, was my oldest daughter. She was born with an electric personality, that was apparently solar-powered. As a highly selective eater, there were days when I swore she lived on water and sunshine, yet she had more energy than anyone I had ever met. As a willowy second grader, she would do most of her homework standing up. This tall drink of water would spin like a top, after she completed each problem, her honey brown hair spinning out in all directions like light rays from the shooting star that she was.

 On the other hand, Chloe at four, lived a deeply imaginary interior life. She could spend hours, sitting on the floor in her favorite seated position. Adult yogis would swoon in envy trying to obtain the same magical posture. You know, where you see kids flop right into that flexible W shape, bending their calves back alongside their thighs, so their ankles are in alignment with their hips and bottom. Chloe was busy creating complex social worlds where Barbies and Polly Pockets had secret super powers. Often when I asked for her attention, it was as if she was coming back into her body, because she had been somewhere else in the stratosphere. Chloe's cherubic pink cheeks were a porcelain contrast to her eyes' dark chocolate liquid pools.

Keith had already spent a career working and
worrying, as he would say, about thousands of
employees and their future retirement benefits, besides
the well-being of his own two sons and grandchildren.
He deserved time to relax and enjoy his life, finally.
Living with a second family isn't an easy feat. I wasn't
confident that Keith was clearly recalling what it was
like to live with young children again. In fact his sons
were adults with babies of their own.

As a tax accountant, I spent my career mitigating
others' risks, certainly not taking them. Also, I saw
family financial conflicts through the lens of people's
tax returns. If people are acting funny, it usually has
something to do with money. Or in Keith's more
elegantly expressed version, "If there is aberrant
behavior, there is usually money involved."

What if I changed everything in my life, and my young
daughters, then Keith realized the error of his ways?
What if he regretted adding three new family
members to his financial picture, and I became his
secret mistake? What if he came to loathe me? My
mind continued to whirl in hypothetical circles over
the next few weeks. I tried out every scenario I could
come up with. I wasn't starting down a path, no
matter how lighthearted at first, without considering
all of the worst-case scenarios. After all that was
what I did in my career every day, noodle through
what-if projections. This was serious, because it

wasn't just my life, it was my two tiny people's future lives too.

Yet I loved the tantalizing opportunity to start an adventure. But also as equally important, his gift of time. I could sit in my own sacred space, imagining different future outcomes and decide for myself.

It was just like the Monte Carlo models, first developed in the 1960's, that we applied to clients' existing portfolios. We would input different facts and investment choices and provide a number of different predicted outcomes to our clients.

The advantage of the Monte Carlo method over its peers, was that it could handle numerous inputs of uncertainty. The more sources of uncertainty, the less predictability exists in a portfolio. This particular computer program was more successful at correctly predicting outcomes, when beta tested against historical fact patterns. This was probably the beginning of the algorithm financial world of today.

And as we all live in the real world, we know that there are millions of inputs that make our personal outcomes impossible to predict, which makes crystal balls and fortune-telling only Holmesian guesswork.

Our choices do decide future outcomes. Your future is definitely in your own hands. Not only that, countless others' futures are impacted by your current choices. So choose wisely. What each of us chooses to do now, changes the future world as we will come to know it, one massively grand Monte Carlo model for sure. I felt myself standing on my own decisive cliff, was I going to make my personal leap of faith, or not?

~ Consider possible Outcomes
before making Serious Moves ~

THE CENTER LINE

~ When Adversity presents itself,
we all Revert to our Center ~

Over the years, I have often heard Keith say, "When
things get tough, everyone returns to their center line."
When I would ask him what exactly did that mean, he
would reply, "Yes, we all can effect changes in our
exterior characteristics, but when confronted with
adversity, we mostly return home to whatever core
values we each hold dear. It is really difficult to break
free from what feels familiar, especially when
circumstances get tough."

When I think back to the early days in our relationship,
I can now see how this adage applied to me. My
comfort zone was to mitigate risk as possible from
situations. Keith's offer to begin a more serious
relationship was definitely far outside my risk-adverse
comfort zone. In contrast, Keith appeared to be a
fearless warrior. In my mind's eye, I saw him armed
with a machete hacking his way through under-brush
in a jungle somewhere far away from my corporate
shared office. This amazing set of circumstances with

Keith felt just like a bungee jump into the Grand Canyon. Pure exhilaration and terror all at once.

 I knew there was only one way I could stray so far from my own comfort zone, and take this leap of faith. It would only be, if Keith and I stood shoulder to shoulder. But, there it was. What if I started down this path of rebooting my life, and Keith withdrew from the field? What would I do then?

Over the next few weeks, I attempted to return to my normal life, driving around the disorganized streets of Atlanta visiting my airline executives to deliver financial planning advice and tax services. Thomas Wolfe's applicably titled novel, *You Can't Go Home Again,* came to mind. Or as I say, once you've had a taste of what can be, you can't return to not knowing. I felt myself edging further and further out onto the ledge, looking down into the canyon, watching birds circling beneath my feet, wondering if I was brave enough to jump.

I sat in teacher conferences, prepared peanut butter and jelly sandwiches and input the never-ending march of timesheets into perpetuity. I meditated on the Teacher's words in Ecclesiastes, "Meaningless, meaningless, everything is meaningless." I thought on Keith's numerous teachable moments, and continued to hear his reverberant advice ringing in my ears.

There was a small guest room on the main floor of this newly constructed home for which we didn't have a specific use. In my new found freedom as a single parent, for the first time in my adult life, I didn't have to negotiate any compromises in domestic matters. So, in one of my attempts to mitigate risk for Hannah and Chloe through both the move to Atlanta and divorce repercussions, I turned the extra space into an Art Room. I threw a bunch of moving canvases over the installed carpet, purchased two easels and art supplies. We drew a center line down the center of the room on the canvas, so each daughter had exactly half of the wall space to exhibit their art.

When I returned home each evening from work, I would often find the girls' painting away under Lizzie's watchful eye each in their own way. Hannah was prolific with her brushes. She maintained a fast and furious approach with the aim of papering her entire side of the room as quickly as possible. In contrast, Chloe would sit with one paper on her easel, solemnly contemplating each brushstroke before completion.

One early evening, I sat at Hannah's easel after her abrupt departure for the playroom regions downstairs in the walk-out basement. At first I was only keeping Chloe company, but then I responded to that creative spark that all humans have whether it is suppressed or expressed. For the first time in years, I picked up some charcoal and began sketching the view that stretched out beneath our window.

If you have visited Atlanta, you will know that the rolling hills can be surprisingly steep. In our home's case, we were perched on the crest of a hill in a newly built subdivision of suburbia. We looked down almost a hundred feet onto the curling neighborhood road, cleanly framed by newly poured concrete curbing. The soft, flickering gaslight lamplight powered by natural gas on our neighbors' front porches, was quite hauntingly charming.

Perhaps, because I took time and allowed that creative spark expression, albeit sporadically and latently, I began to allow myself latitude from my rigid center line of risk aversion. I began to get comfortable looking at things in a new way. Finally, I got to this place, if you don't try, you will never know. I came to feel that it would be a bigger regret for my future self. If I didn't go and find out if this would work. It would linger as an unanswered question the rest of my life. Of one thing I was sure. I was not asking for anyone else's advice. This was going to be an experiment between Keith and me. I didn't want anyone else's opinions muddying up my decision process, and as we all know everyone has something to say about how others should live.

Shortly thereafter, I sat in yet another interminable traffic jam on Atlanta's I-85, I plugged in my tangled Blackberry's phone charger into my Honda Odyssey's cigarette lighter. Back in the day, one of the cool things about the Blackberry was that it was akin to reading braille. You knew where your fingers sat on the keyboard, so you didn't have to look at the phone at all. Compare this to today's smart phone soft keys, or in this case dumb phones. Often, when driving down an urban street today, it looks like people's heads are going to pop-off like heavy headed dandelions from juicy stems. We are all so busy looking at smartphone keyboards, vigilantly attempting to manage misspelled auto-correction, that we lose a few along the way as they stumble into oncoming traffic.

I loved that Honda mini-van too. I could pack and carry the world in there, just like my purse! The most optimally efficient Mom car designed up to that point. As I crawled through traffic, I listened to a favorite pop hit of the day, *1985*, sung by Bowling for Soup. Like many mid-career women with young children, the lyrics were about me. I graduated high school in 1985, and many of us dreamed of being the next discovered "face" for an MTV video. Just like the song's cynical lyric referencing Tawny Kitaen on the hood of Whitesnake's car . Then suddenly one day you look up, and you realize that was twenty-five years ago! The smart aleck lyrics made me laugh again, as I hummed along, "When did Ozzy become an actor? Where's the mini skirt made of snake skin?"

Maybe that day, it was the combination of musical social commentary on my life and the metropolitan traffic snarl that gave me the courage that finally goaded me into action to make that fated call to Palm

Beach. I don't know. But I had decided. I needed to find out for myself. With hands shaking, I dialed up Keith's cell phone down in Florida, mumbling something like there's no time like the present.

~ Tap into your Creative Spark, who knows what unknown Horizon will Appear? ~

CONNECTION

~ *You will never Know, if you don't Ask* ~

I wasn't sure if he would answer, it was cocktail hour in Palm Beach. At this time of day, I already knew how he and his dear friend, Hamlin, enjoyed to meet after a round of golf to discuss their scores, the day's politics and tell some yarns. After a few rings, I heard Keith's vibrating Baritone:

"What a pleasant surprise, Erica! I wasn't expecting to hear from you. How's Atlanta treating you?" Keith's voice trumpeted over the cell phone towers into my left ear. This was back in the day before bluetooth, car pairing and cell phone legislation.

"Keith Elliott!" I loved to start out phone calls this way, enunciating the end syllable of a name like a statement of fact. Somehow, I realized by using both the first and last name of a person, it was a sign of valued recognition. There was only one of them, a unique universe unto themselves. I continued:

"I wasn't expecting to raise you this time of day!" I couldn't help using one of Keith's stock phrases as a subtle reminder that I loved his style of phrasing.

"Raise you" can be a gambling or bartering term, that stayed alive longer in the South than it did in urban centers.

"It's so good to hear your voice," I continued. The words lilted off my tongue in a sing song kind of rhythm and when I said the word, voice, mine was climbing the octave scale. This expression of personal greeting, was something I heard my Dad say over the course of my life, so it was ingrained in me. Pop meant it too, every time he was on the phone with a church parishioner. I think it was more personal than, 'so good to hear from you'. As we are all products of our environment, I had co-opted this particular expression as my own.

But when it came to Keith, the phrase, so good to hear your voice, took on a whole new level of meaning. His mellifluous baritone, just rolled down my ear canals like velvet. The little auditory cilia hairs stood up on end and just vibrated against their tectorial membrane. The vibration felt just like a cat does when it's purring as you pet it. I had never had this kind of physical reaction to someone's voice before. That auditory eighth cranial nerve to my brain was vibrating at some insane rate, so I could barely inhale. With my heart pulsating out of my chest, I forgot all of my planned sophisticated introductory comments, so I stumbled from a standing start with:

"If you have a minute, I wanted to respond to your offer from a few weeks ago. As you recommended, I've been thinking on it pretty hard since then, and I've reached a decision I'd like to share with you."

I could hear the tone of surprise in Keith's voice, as he asked Hamlin for a moment as he stepped outside. They were hanging out at Cucina, one of their favorite haunts in Palm Beach. It is a great local bar run by a large family, with lots of positive energy. As one would expect, it was also pretty loud. So emotional, serious conversations were best conducted outside, leaning against the cool concrete wall, away from the pulsating music and boisterous customers.

Once Keith was settled, I continued, "I don't know how to start this, so I'm just gonna say it. I've thought really hard about your offer to get together. I loved that you gave me the gift of time to go off and think about it for myself. I am nervous because of all of the complicated factors in our lives, but I can't stop thinking about you. I am touched that you want to even try. Since we live in two different states, I really don't know how we would do this, especially with my full-time professional and personal commitments. But you are the best person I've ever met, and I don't want to look back on my life and regret that we didn't take a chance for discovery."

My initial foray, was met with complete silence on Keith's end of the phone, so I began to panic a bit as I stumbled on with an attempt at humor:

"That being said, you might have spent the last few weeks deciding that you were momentarily insane, and prefer to take your offer off the table, which I would completely understand."

Keith's reserve continued on the other end of the phone, which I found unnerving, because there were no tells to read. I knew that this was a great trait in a board room for an erudite executive. It gave one the ability to process proposals, without giving up any power or hints. But in the arena of personal romance, it was downright terrifying. Is this what men went through all the time, when they asked a woman to dinner? I was quickly garnering a new found respect for the opposite sex in this regard. As I nervously rambled on, I felt sure, that Keith was going to reply in the negative with something innocuous such as, "Erica, I had a great time, but you are right, it's just way too complicated for me at this time in my life. Why don't you just stick to being my tax accountant."

When I finally shut up, Keith's vocals sounded like the engine of a 1972 Barracuda roaring to life (my favorite muscle car of all time). Clearing his throat:

"Erica, as I told you before, you are the most fascinating woman I've met in a long time. You have all the votes. So, girl, if you are waiting on me you are backing up! Now it's all about execution!"

With a breath of relief, inwardly I thought, oh my word! I suddenly wasn't sure if I could handle this hurricane gale-force wind's full frontal attack. I felt like I was run over. I heard James Taylor's nasally twang as he sang his love ballad about a steam roller rolling all over me. How applicable.

By this time, I had pulled off an exit ramp, and sat in a gas station looking at my calendar. We made some plans around my existing work travel. In a few weeks, I expected to attend a tax conference in Orlando, so I volunteered to make the first visit to Palm Beach as a boondoggle off that work trip. I would take a puddle jumper from Orlando down to West Palm Beach, for one night away from the conference. I didn't feel so bad, stealing a night away from interminable networking as opposed to adding on another night away from my daughters.

~ Your future resides in your Choices,
so pick wisely, especially when taking Risks ~

TRADEWINDS BLOWING

~ *Double Check when you don't believe your Gut the First Time around* ~

So, it was déjà vu, as we met again at the Palm Beach Grill where we picked up as if it was yesterday. As before, we lingered and closed down the restaurant. It was repeat lightning in a bottle. How did this happen? Neither of us wanted this to end. I noticed Keith pulled what looked like two ticket stubs out of his left breast shirt pocket, and was turning them over in his powerful, square hands. What were they? Movie tickets?

 I feigned ignorance, as I fiddled with my Blackberry deleting some of the hundreds of emails that perpetually cluttered my inbox. I loved the dense font on the Blackberry, similar to today's Kindle density. The speed of its roller ball to move through the screens was my kind of efficiency, I could stop that thing on a dime.

Keith came out of his reverie, and asked, "Would you like to attend the second half of the Palm Beach Pops' concert at the Kravis Center? I have season tickets, and I haven't made it yet this season. We've already missed the first part, but they are probably at intermission now, we could catch the last act?" The unspoken question of continuing our time together hung in the air between us.

Keith's hesitation was also probably a recognition of our age gap. There was that generation that lived between Keith and me, the infamous Baby Boomers. As a Gen X woman who came of age in the Eighties, I didn't necessarily care about the American Songbook, the wheelhouse of the Pops. But at that point, I would have followed Keith anywhere. If he said, he wanted to go help the local enviro-enthusiasts save turtle eggs on the Midtown beach at the stroke of midnight, I would have rolled off my stockings and joined in the quixotic hunt.

It still felt like the first night together, the first time our eyes met, but it only felt so much stronger, as only Bryan Adams could belt out in his *Please Forgive Me* hit. How could this be? This was only the third time we had laid eyes on each other.

Just as before, the elven valet appeared with a flourish with Keith's roadster convertible, from five spots away. We drove West over the bridge also known as OTB to utilize the local acronym. Keith regaled me with "Only in Palm Beach" stories as we continued towards the Kravis Center.

Keith began with some of the cartographical facts. As we learned in history class, geography shapes history. Many wars were fought over embankments, river rights and ocean passages. And this was the local case here as well. The only difference being that the wars were more legislative, billions of dollars in real estate tax collections hard won at the ballot box.

The Townies, otherwise self-described as Palm Beachers, lived the farthest East on the skinny barrier island holding the Town of Palm beach. The island stretches about twenty miles North to South with the Atlantic Ocean on its Eastern shore. The intracoastal waterway is on the town's Western back, separating it from the City of West Palm Beach. In contrast, the big city's urban sprawl spread west for miles, creeping towards the Everglades. Today, the massive Lake Okeechobee is prominent on every map of the United States, documented daily on the weather map of each USA Today.

Even though the Kravis Center was only a mile or so West of the Town of Palm Beach and the ocean, Keith described how Palm Beachers would funnily, sometimes snootily, say "Do we have to go off the island?" Keith snorted:

"I-ahhh call it Fantasy Island because it's often a load of horse-sh*t!" Keith ribbed with good natured commentary. While we laughed together in an easy

camaraderie, again I pleasured in hearing his Southern
drawl unfurl alongside his emotion, as he relaxed.

Visions of the old school prime time show, *Fantasy
Island*, flashed across my eyes. As usual, I loved to
mentally categorize the hypocrisy of Hollywood. How
they derided us regular working people with our
supposed prejudice, as they produced shows based on
stereotypes of race, gender and little people. The late
Herve Villechaize's voice as Tattoo singing "Da Plane"
was iconic. Yet this little person was apparently fired
by Hollywood for demanding an equal salary with his
regular sized co-star, if you can believe the tabloids
and Wikipedia. Villechaize became the ungrateful
villain's face in the supermarket checkout line. I
returned from my mental pilgrimage into the
inequities of celebrity stardom or stardoom, my own
catty play on words. I picked up on a new interesting
story-line Keith was developing:

"When I was in college, I managed the bar at a kind of
dude ranch up in Lake George, New York called
Sunnybrook Acres. You know, horses and stuff."

At this point the drawbridge started flashing and going
up which led a string of annoyed swears from Keith's
lips for being further delayed from our cultural goal.
Yet unknown to us, it was the first of many future
bridge openings that I would try to avoid, and would
subsequently sit through when I lost the race with
time.

As we sat dwelling on lost time, I thought about the mysterious poetry of Samuel T. Coleridge's allegory, *Time, Real and Imaginary.* The poem is a word picture of a sister and brother running along a plateaued mountain top with arms outstretched like sails. The sister ran backwards to keep an eye on her brother. He raced blind, not knowing if he was winning or losing their never- ending race. So, does the sister symbolize the real or imaginary time? And what the heck is imaginary time anyway?

It was a poem that I held as a secret against my own heart since I found it in some pages as a prepubescent youth. I would write then type it out in my most important papers to keep it close to me. Hoping that one day I would be enlightened by its physical proximity if not actual understanding. As I left my mental time tableau, I asked:

"What? I thought Dude ranches were out West somewhere, like in *City Slickers,* the Billy Crystal movie," I responded.

Belatedly, I realized that I had lost that errant tube of lipstick again in my purse that doubled as a briefcase. Surreptitiously, I started digging around in the black cavernous space, trying not to garner too much attention to my lack of feminine attention to detail.

Keith replied, "I know, being from a little pee wee town in the backwoods of South Carolina, I had no ideeee-ahhh either that there were dude ranches in New York. New York was a far away place, almost a fairy tale land. As a matter of fact, I was probably one of the few in my little town of Abbeville, South Carolina that actually went to New York as a child."

With surprise I asked, "How did that happen? I know you told me your Momma, Sarah Belle, raised you all by herself after she divorced your Dad, which totally blows my mind. What a brave woman to not put up with any nonsense in the early 1940's during the war, to go off and raise you herself. That was just not done."

With a bit of surprise Keith continued, "Yah know, you are so right. But to answer your question, Grand-Daddy was my Mom's Dad. He and my Dad worked for the railroad. My Dad got me a family rail pass so I could ride the rails to New York City with him."

In my Philly slurred slang, I asked, "Whuddya mean? Ya mean your Dad WORKED with your Mom's Dad and her brothers after she divorced him? How did that go?" This was an important point to me, as I was still reeling from my own divorce pains.

With a bit of surprise, Keith confirmed, "Yes, they somehow figured it out. They all knew how tough my Mom was, as the only girl amongst the four siblings. They still all got out of her way when she was mad. I think they knew not to mess with her after she had

enough of my Father's frivolous ways. And my
Grand-Daddy was a HUGE man for his time, six -
foot five inches or so. I think all the men in mah
family figured out how to work with each other, so
they could provide for their families. After all it was
during World War II, and they were all working for the
railroad. Their jobs were all war-effort imperative jobs.
They moved troops and supplies, so while many
children around me were suffering, we always had
food on the table and all the men worked."

Wow, how forward thinking this family was from this
tiny town in South Carolina. I was building a vision of
this amazing family in the Mayberry town of Abbeville
in my mind. Keith mentioned that his hometown was
actually featured in the Julia Roberts romance slash
psychopath movie *Sleeping with the Enemy* , an
oxymoron if there ever was one. I had a mental flash
of Julia riding on the bus through the town's square,
so quaint and wonderful! As I was trying to recall the
famous actor that played the psycho-killer, the
drawbridge started to descend into a road once more.
As Keith placed the roadster back into drive, he
rambled on:

"I got to see Mickey Mantle play for the Yankees, if
you can believe that. Mah Dad used some of his
railcar passes, so we could travel to New York City for
a special treat. I was there when they played a famous
double header against the Chicago White Sox. It was
a double win for me, cuz Nellie Fox was the second

basemen, my favorite player cuz that wuz mah position too."

"Why was that day so famous?" I asked.

"Well, I was real little, so ah know he was pretty young in his career at the time and causing quite a sensation. But that night, The Mick came the closest to hitting a homerun out of Yankee Stadium, as far as I know that is still true today. The Yankee stadium is huge and tall, unlike the Cubs stadium in Chicago, where kids stand in the street to catch a baseball. But that night, Mantle came the closest ever. He hit two homeruns. The first one went thirty rows deep in the very top section. The second one, hit the top edge of the stadium. I can see myself in my mind's eye entering through the stadium's gates with my Dad. I didn't want to miss any part of the game, so I almost peed my pants! It was an amazing memory for a newspaper boy from South Carolina."

"Anyways, so when I went to work in New York while I was in college it was a whole different thing. Sunnybrook Acres was a resort in Lake George, New York, up in the Adirondacks. So, I can imagine it was pretty dramatic for a New York City family to drive out and see an actual cowboy on a horse. *Mah* friend, Dallas, recruited me to be up there as a bar waiter *thah* first summer. But before that, we also grew up in Greenwood together; we were both newspaper boys for the Index Journal. We went way back."

I was chuckling. As is often the case, when we know people when we are young, we really know them, then we really trust them, because of all these many data points. So what was up between Keith and me? We both were so comfortable with each other as if we'd spent our whole lives together, but we had very few hours together. How could this be? Very mysterious.

Keith was continuing his storyline, "Dallas was head bartender and had run the bar the previous year. I-ahh tell you what, anything was better than going back to work on the road sign crew on the steaming asphalt of South Carolina. Now that was back breaking work. I was ready for a new summer job."

With a touch of sarcasm I laughingly added, "I am sure it was difficult to choose between ditch digging and working at a summer resort serving drinks working along side pretty young women. But what did your Mom say? I'm sure she didn't want you going to New York for the summer!"

"I think because Dallas had already gone up there the summer before, and was successful, helped my Mom be comfortable with it. Besides it was good money. Anyways, much to mah surprise, after about a week, the owner, Ken Pohl, fired Dallas' ass for some disagreement. Ken was sumpin else. If he didn't like you, he would call you up to his trailer, which served as his summer housing and work office. At the end of each season, he and his wife would drive back home to Miami for the winter."

"Now, Ken made all of his money between Fourth of July and Labor Day. His guests were mostly Italians and Jews from Brooklyn and the Bronx, as well as some Canadiens driving down over the border from Quebec. Therefore, the surprise firing was a pretty risky move on Ken's part, he was already in his short summer season. He needed to make hay while the sun was still shining, in effect. I had only been there about a week, when Mr. Pohl asked me if I knew how to mix cocktails. If so, I could be head bartender."

With a dramatic pause, Keith continued his tale, "Now I had never mixed drinks in mah life, but I'd been watching the whole time I was there, so I replied, 'Give me two weeks,' and that was it!"

~ Don't be afraid to try New Things,
who knows where it will Lead You ~

SOME SET OF WHEELS

~ Say what You Mean ~

When we arrived at the striking Kravis Center, it was lit up like a Christmas tree. The dramatic entrance to the modern building was floor to ceiling glass that reached upwards for two to three stories. Through the window panes, one could view the beautiful massive chandeliers, burning like constellations in planetariums we've all visited in our elementary school days. I remember numerous trips to Philadelphia's Franklin Institute craning our necks to see artificial constellations and walking through a papier-mache giant human's heart.

But in this seething mass of humanity, there was a battalion of valets out in full force, as opposed to one or two at the more intimate restaurant settings. They were scooting around cars in an intricate dance, assisting the legions of sparkling guests. Now this was before Andy Cohen's T.V. based *Housewives* in multiple American cities. So, the array of pumped up lips and botox-ed foreheads was definitely disconcerting in their proliferation. Besides the augmented crowd, I was also intrigued by how many of the patrons were replete with canes and walkers. I was impressed. Not only with the alacrity of the valets, but the sheer soul force of these more delicate elderly individuals. Nothing was going to stop them from expanding their minds' horizons and experiences, not spinal stenosis, or the like. I hoped I lived as long and as fully. They were inspiring to say the least.

As Keith appeared at my elbow, we entered together and were presented with two flutes of champagne as we snaked our way through crowds towards the auditorium doors. As we entered, I walked ahead of Keith down the steps. Now at this point, we were on a date, but we were officially client and financial professional. Therefore, picking out an outfit seemed nigh on impossible for this momentous occasion. When I was packing for this trip, I had settled on a black shift type dress from my Jones of New York working career woman collection. It had some feminine pink tiny flowers embroidered on it, versus hard core straight up business. I had some kind of pink matching scarf. As I was still from the chilly North, I wore black stockings and a medium black heel. Down here in the steamy South, I quickly realized that no one wore hose of any kind, but I was used to being the outlier. I hadn't belonged anywhere for a long time. Besides the air conditioning in Florida was like an ice box, I was pretty sure I was going to need the extra layer of insulation.

As I walked ahead of Keith towards our seats, as directed by the hostess, I could actually feel Keith's eyes burning a hole through my skin. By the time we sat down, Keith was visibly affected. His fair Scottish skin was flushed pink. He said in a failed attempt at a whisper, "Girl, you got some set of wheels on you."

I don't blush easily, but my face was on fire, yet again this man rendered me speechless. Oh, to be so brave and willing to speak one's own mind. In contrast, I would spend hours in mental exercise working out what I needed to say. He just came right out with it.

Suddenly, Keith leaned forward and looked across me to the couple seated on my left. In that booming voice, Keith belted out, "Caroll is that you? Let me introduce you to my tax accountant, Erica. Erica, this is Carroll Peacock and his wife. Carroll is a premier architect here in town."

With that the genteel couple both shook hands with me as Carroll joked, "But you don't look like a tax accountant." Now in the beginning of my budding service career, this aside created all kinds of consternation for me, how I didn't really belong. I was an interloper. Sometimes, it was meant as a nasty dig, that you can't be both a fairly attractive woman and also have a brain.

But as I gained my own technical confidence, I got more comfortable in my own skin. It was okay to be different, in fact it was a good thing, so I began to embrace it. Therefore, with a broad grin, I returned with my own practiced repartee:

"Why thank you! Because this is my disguise!"

With that we all laughed, and Mr. Peacock talked about some of his career projects. The music began, and I tried as subtly as possible to cuddle up my near six-foot frame, closer to Keith's shoulder. I could feel his body heat just radiating straight through his navy blue blazer. As the Floridian air conditioning blasted down upon us, the goosebumps on my Mediterranean derived skin stood up in indignant protest. Wow I felt so protected by this powerful man's presence, so calming. When was I ever calm? My early morning return flight to Orlando seemed a hypothetical event happening to someone else. For the first time in my life, I felt like I belonged, wrapped around Keith's elbow, that felt like the limb of an oak tree. As the music soared to its ending crescendo, I was nestled in this radiant blanket of heat, both actual and emotional.

Afterwards, we cued up in the VIP valet lane. Keith was growling with impatience that we had to wait at all when his car was parked ten feet away. Again, I found this to be a hilarious contrast to my own personal history. I recalled one particular night after a Philadelphia Flyers' game, where my rangy tall Pop decided that he was going to run his three children into the ground like a Navy Seal Team Six episode. As we raced to our car so we could "beat the traffic" onto the I-95 interstate to get home. What were we going to win besides a hopeful continuance on life?

After we curled into the innards of that silver bullet of a car, Keith asked, "I don't know about you, but if you would like, we can sit in my backyard by the pool. It's a beautiful night still, but only if you feel comfortable. Because as I told you before, Erica, you have all the votes."

What an endearing expression! I was born with a neurotic safety gauge. I took no chances that put me in danger, ever. I always played safe rather than sorry. Never in my life had I put myself in a position where I had to trust a man to behave. But here was another first. I trusted this man. It was in the tone of his voice, his sincerity, his small signs of respect. Secretly my heart already knew if given the chance, I would follow him anywhere. But my mind still practiced doubt and denial.

~ Don't be afraid to Ask, it is Then you Find what you are Looking for ~

BETWEEN THE HEDGES

~ Pause to Enjoy the unexpected Beauty
in each Journey ~

I interrupted my internal dialogue and readily accepted Keith's offer to not yet call it quits. After my immediate agreement, we drove East, back onto the island of Palm Beach. We drove for a few blocks through a small retail area before turning left to enter the residential North End, using the locals' colloquial expression. We continued our drive North for another mile or two. This point of entry was clearly delineated on County Road, by a canopy of massive ficus trees which lined both sides of the road. They arched away overhead creating a tunnel effect, thick enough to actually block out radio and cell phone tower signals. It reminded me of entering spiraling naves in ancient churches, where the air is cool and sacred under the protective shrouded space.

As we came through the trees, we were still in this emerald green fairy land of foliage. I caught my breath over the beautiful hedges, carved into unique shapes hiding home after home along the way. The verdant green bushes towered overhead, each one at least ten feet tall. Even though it was dark, their luminescence still shimmered. There were no bricks and mortar to contrast against the evergreen, as each home was sheltered behind their manicured privacy hedges. They were like rings of elven green soldiers camouflaging their residential charges. The only place I had seen this much urban gardening in one place was the massive acreage of Fairmount Park in the heart of Philadelphia. Or as the Philly-phile that I still am, the Philadelphia Flower Show, the oldest, biggest and best. Yet this was different, because of the massive continual effort to maintain these manicured, neatly contrived shapes. It was more in line with a reminiscent but more random emulation of the gardens at Versailles.

Suddenly there was a sharp curve in the road, and the Atlantic Ocean appeared in front of us, its indigo waves rolling. She was streaked with silver moonlight cutting a path across her waves. A line of poetry that I wrote in my younger years rolled through my mind,

"Days are like islands I travel along, one at a time down a chain to the sea…"

I needed to add a line about the moon, I only had one about the sun reflecting back. Here it was the moon just vibrating off the inky dark waters. Hmmmm..

As we rounded another bend in, we were back between the hedges, and shortly thereafter turned onto

Tradewind Drive, the street's name couldn't be more apropos. I recognized the street name already from Keith's tax return, which I found amusing.

Another client of mine would joke that I knew more about him than his own family after preparing their taxes for years. And in some odd ways it is true. Birthdays, social security numbers, addresses scrolled across my brain's screen as I worked and sometimes when I slept.

We rolled through more emerald shrouds of these dramatic hedges, and pulled into Keith's semi-circular driveway. As the convertible's engine purred to a halt, we could hear the sounds of the tropical night all around us, as Keith closed the hardtop on the convertible. Two majestic Royal Palms rose through the center of a hedge, and the winds rustled through their palm fronds. From half a block away, one could still hear the murmur of the ocean beckoning us to return.

From all the years of academic schoolwork and laptop keyboarding, my neck didn't like to look upwards too much anymore. So, I rested the back of my skull on the headrest, before the roof completely closed to catch a glimpse of a sky normally hidden from me by the halo effect of urban lights. It was as if the Milky Way was lighting the way on our new journey.

Our galaxy's guest appearance, reminded me of the new book that my client-friend, Janis, had recommended to me, *River of Souls* by Dr. Brian Weiss. It was blowing open a new passage way in my mind, this clinical hypno-therapist's documentation of his patients' case studies. Apparently, his clients had re-experienced some of their past lives while in a trance-like state. These surprise appearances were shocking to Dr. Weiss as his planned regressions were supposed to identify an early traumatic childhood experience as the cause of a specific phobia. But much to the doctor's surprise, his patients, of their own accord, started jumping into other lifetimes, to bring up a traumatic experience from the prior life. Once the past life trauma was re-lived, his patient would subsequently activate a spontaneous healing and free themselves from a current debilitating phobia.

It was all quite amazing to read about, particularly as an open-minded skeptic. Maybe this was why Keith felt so hauntingly familiar and home to me? Had we been together before? What a fascinating idea!

~ Pay Attention to how People and Places make you Feel ~

EXPECT THE UNEXPECTED

~ *Don't place others in Boxes you Create* ~

As we entered Keith's beautiful Bermuda style home,
we walked across cool white Travertine marble floors
We entered a smartly remodeled kitchen that would
have made any chef purr with delight. As he proudly
showed off the new finishes, I was pleasantly
surprised, that Keith was a man that loved to cook!

In contrast, I had no current interest, probably due to
exhaustion. By the time I came home from work,
hugged my daughters, the last thing I wanted to do
was cook. I was happy with a bowl of cereal and a
cup of tea.

As we continued our kitchen tour, Keith opened
smoothly gliding drawers, with special kitchen tools
nestled in their own homes, Keith said, "Nanny was
what I called *mah* grandmother Maizie. Now she
could cook anything that my Granddaddy caught or
shot. Ahhh remember her with her one black iron
skillet. Every morning she would drop a dab of bacon
grease in there, and make the best biscuits. I would
shove them in my coat pockets, as I jumped on *mah*
bike to ride to school. To this day, the best biscuits I

ever had. Those sum biches were two inches thick. You broke um apart and they were steaming hot. Then you would spread em with a bit of honey or jam, oh mah gahd."

I reflected on the wide arching path that Keith's life must have taken from that childhood of a simpler time to the glamorous Palm Beach kitchen where we now stood. As I did my mental comparisons, Keith opened this beautiful lovely wooden door just off of his open concept kitchen. The door led to a wine "cellar" that held about one thousand bottles of wine in a floor to ceiling closet, a four by six-foot space. The wooden door was so lovely, it was hand carved wooden relief, depicting medieval monks in various stages of grape growing, wine making and enjoying the literal fruits of their labor. So humorous and unique at the same time. Technically, it was not a cellar since it was above ground. Due to the high level of the water table in Florida, it is quite difficult to have a basement, since it would be a constant source of structural hazard to a homeowner. His wine cellar was really a temperature-controlled room, with a specialized air conditioner designed for wine that was vented out through the garage.

Keith appeared with a bottle of wine from his cherished collection that he had developed over decades in his life. As he reached into a wooden box, that held a specialized wine-opener, his baritone kicked up a notch in volume, "Anyone can spend a whole lotta money for a great bottle of wine, but Ah like to do my homework. It is sumpin' else if you can find a great bottle of wine for a great value! Now that's something special!"

In contrast, I knew there was red and there was white wine, and that was about the extent of it. With a big grin I teased, "Well, I would have to say that not everyone CAN spend a whole lotta money on a bottle of wine. But from my perspective, since I have no idea what I'm doing in the wine department, I can find a low-cost bottle of wine, and it tastes like what I call wedding wine."

As Keith used the "rabbit-ears" designed by some genius engineer, to pull out the cork in one full-swoop, he started to laugh, "Wedding wine? What, like Jesus turning the water into wine?"

"No, I mean like I am at someone's wedding, and they are pouring the cheapest wine possible, and it tastes like I'm licking the shoe polish off my shoe."

Now it was Keith's turn to laugh, as he poured out a dark blackberry colored wine into two tall stemmed glasses. I continued:

"Wine is like taxes there is so much detail, how do you keep them all straight?"

Keith started to explain how for the past thirty years he had studied Wine Spectator and other journals in his spare time. Then he would work with his local wine store to help him acquire some of the value buys that he had read about.

"Well, like anything else, you make some big picture earmarks as memory guides. For example, hands down, 1997 is a great California vintage. You'd have to be deaf, dumb and blind NOT ta make great wine in that year. So, you have a pretty good shot to hit the broad side of a barn if you bought a ninety-seven."

At the time, I was a vino-neophyte, so I didn't know what wine Keith opened. But the arresting flavors were a shocking charge to the senses. It was definitely a rich, chewy dark red, that made my taste buds tingle. It was not like any wedding wine that I had had in my short life. As I swished it around the sides of my mouth like a little fish bowl, I could feel different areas of my mouth activating, so alive! Then after I swallowed, I could still feel this residual reaction across my tongue. When asked, Keith talked about the tannins in the wine that are part of a wine's molecular makeup.

"Wow, it's like a chemistry experiment." I commented, as we walked back through the great room heading towards the backyard. This made Keith laugh at the implied reference to one of his dual studies, an Economics major but almost another in Chemistry. How ironic. Just as my career in taxes chose me, it appeared that Keith's destiny chose him. For his two lines of studies served him well, as he spent most of his career as a financial executive in the chemical industry, killing two birds with one stone in effect.

"Yes, when we swirl wine around in the glass or use a decanter, we are 'oxidizing the esters' in technical chemical language or in other words we are getting oxygen into the wine so it escalates the taste. It comes alive," as Keith took another sip of his wine.

We paused our journey towards the pool to admire some of Keith's artwork hanging in the great room. Keith was describing his personal interaction with the famed artist, Peter Max, when acquiring an original rendition of his Umbrella Man. Suddenly, I was overwhelmed with all-encompassing emotion, yes I was coming alive. I saw myself as a mythical genie springing forth into fresh air for the first time in years. I started humming Christina Aguilera's *Genie in a Bottle* lyrics in my own tone-deaf way.

I had something in common with the wine in my hand. We were both waking up from our Rip Van Winkle bottled-up sleep. Fresh trade winds were blowing through my soul.

~ Be open to try New Things,
who knows where they may Take You ~

POOLSIDE

~ When you find Beauty, Pause to really See it ~

Like that very first night, we continued to include Jack
Johnson in our evening's plans, when Keith turned on
the outside speakers. Jack played his recorded concert
for us out under those beautiful stars. Soft landscape
lights lit the palm trees from each of their bases.
Shooting light through the palm fronds from beneath,
their shadows dancing across the white stucco garden
walls beyond the lights' grasp.

Poolside, we settled into two platform rocking chairs. I
stared down into the depths of the crystalline pool.
Its surface rippled with the ocean breezes, while the
underwater lights made the water come alive with
reflected movement. It was as if an invisible hand was
stirring the pot. I thought of my childhood heroine,
Anne of Green Gables, talking to dryad water spirits, all
of her imaginary friends. It felt like the wind through
the trees was whispering to me, open your heart.

~ Slow down and Listen
to the small Voice within You ~

BURGUNDY

~ There can be Multiple Levels of Meaning in things ~

"You were talking about buying someone's collection of Burgundy wine. How did that happen? Besides, what does Burgundy actually mean? Obviously, it is a shade of red, but what more did it reference in the wine world?"

I loved how comfortable it was to pepper Keith with as many questions as I liked. He enjoyed it and didn't laugh at my ignorance in his field of expertise. My goal after all was to learn everything about everything. And I was standing in the middle of a new field of unexplored territory, my favorite kind.

"Well first Burgundy is a geographic region in France that mostly produces wine made from the specific grape Pinot Noir.

"So Burgundy is a place and Pinot Noir is a grape varietal."

"Yes, but in New World wines, such as here in America, often the type of grape is prominently identified on the label, because we don't have the same lengthy history and regulations that Old World wines such as the French have. During the 1970's wine started to become popular in America. In an effort to jump start the wine education of the American public, the actual grape types were listed on each bottle. If it was a blend of grapes, the percentage of each varietal is explicitly spelled out. But this is not true of Old World counterparts. It is what is required in each region, so the type of grape is not listed on the label. In fact, in France, they have…"

I interrupted, "What do you mean? Aren't all Burgundies red? Like in Revlon's Burgundian Red Lipstick?"

"No actually, all grapes produce a white liquid, if the skins are strained off. The depth of color is determined by how long grape skins are left in the wine as it ferments. Besides the length of time, the type of grape varietal also affects the final hue."

As I write this story here in 2019, you may find it surprising that I knew as little about wine as I did. As my Pop was a Preacher Man, we became a dry household pretty early on. Pop spent a lot of time helping alcoholics and addicts recover. He chose not to drink so he would not be a stumbling block to those around him. So, it was just something not in my consciousness. And I knew it was a huge pool of unexplored knowledge. My favorite kind of territory.

As a little girl I do remember our next door neighbor, Mommo Janicki. She made her own home brewed wine in the basement of her Philadelphia row home, back when the local regulators weren't aware that it was their jurisdiction to write you up for these kind of licentious abuses. Mommo was an immigrant from the Old World. She would bring these big gallon wine jugs that looked like orange Gatorade and Welch's Grape Juice over to our house. After taking a sip of that, I labeled wine as a shoe polish. Not much changed as I grew into adulthood. After entering the labor-intensive world of Public Accounting, I didn't have time to sleep let alone try new things. That was something others did, I was interested in earning my own paycheck and retaining my performance-based job on a daily basis.

As my mind returned from the annals of my childhood, I heard Keith switching gears:

"But Erica, to answer the question about the wine collection itself, I must go back to 1975. I had a life-threatening medical situation that put me in the hospital on an emergency basis. Eventually, the thing resulted in a diagnosis on the operating room table called Meckel's Diverticulum. Later my doctors told me I was probably within twenty-four hours of dying, as I was wracked with fever and extraordinary pain. If they hadn't opened me up, they wouldn't have found the infected area. Even then it was the resident surgeon in the room, that had just studied the rare condition in medical school that knew where to look. All of my life, I've had a real respect for doctors. They do stuff that really matters, saving lives."

"The surgery was quite serious and caused me to be out of work for close to three months. My boss, came to see me every day so I didn't get to lay off while I was recovering. I remained mentally engaged in work, which I really appreciated."

"Anyways, while I was in the hospital, I asked for two books, one book on wine and one on photography. I read them both and got very interested in both things. Pretty soon I'd gotten a lot better and back to work for a solid period of time. It was then that I learned that my two co-workers, Dan Burnham and Gene Richards, were big lovers of wine. They liked to buy from Sokolin of New York City and have it shipped directly to where we lived in the western part of the state. That was really the first experience that I ever really had of consequence. We began to buy enough wine between the three of us that we had a truck deliver it to one of our homes. It was probably a total of twenty-five to thirty cases at a time, divided between three homes. That was my first experience with real wine and I had a good time learning about it."

I was still staring down into the crystalline blue swimming pool, as we swirled red wine around in its own little pools of hand blown glass. It struck me how Keith had literally been sitting in death's doorway. Upon his recovery, he had acquired two new creative interests, wine and photography.

It was one of the first times I was aware of this phenomenon: newly acquired interests after visiting with the shadow of death. But it would not be the last. I hadn't yet read *Reality* by the philosopher, Peter Kingsley. The author describes how the ancients artificially created resurrection after a three day period, a rebirth into a higher consciousness. We can choose to ignore our unconscious passions until we are knocked down flat. But upon our return, often we are bearing new gifts.

~ Don't ignore your Creative Side, because it will Find a way to Express Itself ~

WOMEN IN BUSINESS

~ Keep your Mind Open: One can learn many Lessons along the way from Others ~

Without any ado, we got up from our separate chairs and settled into the loveseat glider, in an unspoken compulsion to physically touch. We sat side by side gently swaying in the gloaming night, with the Milky Way still smiling down upon us. It was so natural to feel for Keith's warmth through his shirtsleeve, and gently stroke his forearm with my thumb and index finger as we continued to talk.

It was easy for me to forget the string of interviews that awaited me the next day back in Orlando. I was in the middle of this arduous process of being "put up for partner" to use our internal firm's speech. This was in the early two thousands, when flexible working schedules, working remotely, and women partners were all relative novelties. I still had a checklist of things still missing from my tax partner candidacy package, including the likes of selling more work, creating a larger recurring revenue stream, getting validation from partners in the gargantuan audit and assurance side of the business. This was right after the breathtaking crashes of Enron and WorldCom. It was first the abuse of tax shelters. Then it was sheer fraudulent valuation of companies based on future notional values that were at the crux of these debacles.

My first employer, Arthur Andersen, was now dead. This proud, hundred year old firm, was the lone sacrificial lamb out of all of the financial businesses that profited from their scandalous involvement. Uncle Arthur's spectacular demise was predicted by Paul Volcker, the former chair of the Federal Reserve, in his public passionate plea with his governmental successors to not censure the partnership itself. Instead he argued for the partners that perpetrated the frauds to be individually prosecuted. Otherwise, he pointed out that the effect would be the destruction of the firm's form only. All the partners would just leave and join other accounting firms, or start new ones. In my view along with many others, Volcker argued for the correct outcome. As is often the case, governmental regulators who never worked in private industry don't understand fully the fragility of private institutions. The full chilling impact was just as the author of Ecclesiastes wrote, "we are all like dust in the wind." The firm immediately lost all of its auditing jobs across the globe, because no one wanted an auditor's report from a tainted accounting firm. And like a snap of the fingers, the great diaspora of audit and tax partners began. They fled to distance themselves as much as possible from the crushing censorship on the entity. The entity was gone like a clap of thunder in the night.

It was after this chilling institutional demise, that I was attempting to achieve a tax partnership in one of the several remaining public accounting firms. When I first came out of college, the largest public accounting firms had been known as the Big Eight for a long long time. Probably the most well known was Price Waterhouse, even though it was the smallest. I think this was because they audited the Oscars each year in Hollywood, and therefore their brand seeped more soundly into the public's consciousness. After the death of Arthur Andersen, the remaining firms became known as the Big Four. Cynically, I renamed our coterie the Final Four, because it appeared the federal government had learned one lesson. It was not in the public's best interest to have fewer than four public accounting firms. There would not be enough competition on price and choice of auditing firms and that would be even less if a public good..

I was already operating under the modus operandi to just do my best and good things will come from it. It might be a different path than the elusive partnership. I imagined that night that the other stressed candidates were holed up in their hotel rooms cramming for their big interviews. But that was not my style. I had put years of hard work in, and if that wasn't enough, the heck with it. I sensed the firm's cultural internal battles. I believed in my self-proclaimed premise: if it got into the too hard pile, it meant it wasn't the right fit anyhow. It was time to move on.

Besides, now it suddenly felt like there was a new path opening before me, and apparently it was starting with my heart.

~Do your best and Allow Outcomes to unfold no matter how Surprising they might be ~

A FEMALE PREDECESSOR

~ When you feel forlornly Alone,
Examine others' examples whom Preceded You ~

As I returned from my silent reverie, I felt Keith's
strong arm around my shoulders along the back of the
glider. All felt right with the world. We were still
walking the tightrope of human mating rituals; our
dance was definitely ratcheted up by the intellectual
melding of our minds. One of my favorite
expressions is that everything is connected. This
building physical crescendo between Keith and me,
was definitely fueled by the mental stimulation. This
meeting of the minds was somewhat terrifying in that
it felt like we could be fueling our own forest fire.
Hopefully, we wouldn't burn down a house. With that
thought, images and lyrics from The Talking Heads
video *Burning Down the House* started to scroll through
my mind's screen. "Hold tight.. Here's your ticket
pack your bag, time for jumpin' overboard...fightin'
fire with fire…"

With a savory shiver running up my spine, I snuggled
into Keith's comforting frame, as he picked up the
story of how he met Amy Stamberg. Apparently, she

was a Renaissance pioneering career woman from the 1970's. Not only was she an investment advisor at a world class firm, she was a wine connoisseur. Keith's throaty baritone began:

"During my time in Niagara Falls when I was Assistant Treasurer at Carborundum is when I met Amy. At the time, she was seriously into wine and in fact was the president of one of the fancy New York wine clubs, not sure which one, but probably Tastevin, which specializes in Burgundy wine, her favorite. By this time, I was buying as a collector and I liked to study about it. I met Amy because she was our representative for the Frank Russell company. You've heard of the Russell Indices?"

With a surprised nod of recognition, I responded, "Oh? Yeah! Ya mean like the Russell 2000 Index?"

"Well I knew George Russell, when he was the one running the investment company. He was the founder's grandson. Well, when we hired George and his firm, it was before they launched their indexes that people still use today to track performance in distinctive market segments such as large and small cap growth and value stocks. He was really ahead of the game when he created these broader transparent measurement stick to track performance. Of course today there are more of these around. But anyways, Amy worked with George on our account. We hired them to advise our pension fund regarding asset allocation and picking money managers."

"At Carborundum, I worked with Dan Burnham and Gene Richards in the Finance Department. All three of us were big into buying our own wine allotments. We each rented independent temperature-controlled wine storage units. I had two of them, where I could store six hundred bottles. I took my time only buying what I liked when I thought it was at a value price, and slowly began to fill up my units. I learned a lot from Amy, I would discuss some of the wines that I planned to buy with her. She knew a lot, especially about Burgundies."

"Years later, I got a call from Amy that she was selling her wine collection and wanted to know if I was interested in buying some of it. She had decided to stop drinking altogether. Her Mom had a serious alcohol problem and I think she was concerned about herself too. I asked Amy to fax over her wine inventory list, which she did. And I ended up making an offer on the whole thing, and bought it all. It is Amy's burgundy wines that I still drink today, and in fact we are having some tonight."

I responded, "Wow that is kinda wild to think about. So, Amy was buying these wines twenty some years ago, and here it is coming alive tonight."

Keith was silent and clearly contemplating some maudlin thoughts. He resumed, "It was just a few years later that I called Amy at home because I had a few questions about a wine I was considering purchasing, and Amy's sister answered the phone, which surprised me. It was then that I found out that Amy had been seriously suffering with depression. Apparently, even though she was brilliant professionally she had also suffered significantly in her personal life. The twists and turns included losing her mother to alcohol, then escaping an abusive relationship. But the final straw appeared to be that while she was traveling a pet sitter had neglected her two dogs. Upon her return she found that they had both starved to death. It was then she ingested a whole bottle of Tylenol and took her own life."

That shocked me. We sat in silence for awhile, clasping our hands together, as I could feel Keith's pain for the loss of a brilliant friend to an unnecessary death. It was the first time we mourned a loss like this together, but unfortunately it was not going to be the last. It is a blessing that the future is often hidden from us behind a veil, because if we knew all things at once, it could be too much for us to bear.

With a quick squeeze of Keith's burly hand, I released it. With a small flourish, I picked up my glass of wine and raised it in a toast,

"To Amy. Let us dwell on the good memories of her."

Keith agreed, "We all have flat spots. She was brilliant and yet she secretly suffered. To Amy."

I continued, "Ya know, in my race to career advancement, it is easy to forget that professional acclaim isn't everything. Sitting here, it would be easy to think that Amy had it all, Princeton, The Russell Company, president of a prestigious wine club, but underneath she was living in pain."

With that I could feel Keith's intensity increase in degrees of radiation as he turned towards me. He replied:

"Erica. That is what I've been saying to you. I've had this amazing career and I can't believe the half of it. I've had the privilege to experience so much. But it doesn't mean a whole lot to me anymore to enjoy it alone. I want you in my life, I want to take you to places you've never been and experience things together. I worked so hard for so long. I was so busy. My personal life suffered. I want to start a new life with you by my side."

Before I could respond to this astonishing declaration, I felt Keith's lips cover mine. I was utterly disarmed and rendered speechless, which as you've now surmised is quite an accomplishment in itself.

~ When looking to our Mentors,
Learn from their Successes but more importantly,
their Shortcomings ~

ATLANTA CULTURE SHOCK

~ *Risk and Reward Ratios*
are not always Transparent ~

That night was a game changer. Again that memorable evening had ended in a repeat moment. Keith returned me to my hotel room in his convertible roadster, so I would get some rest before my early flight back to Orlando. I still recall how hollow I felt watching him drive away from me that night. It felt very wrong, and I suddenly became quite sad.

Therefore, it was quite surreal to go interview with a bunch of accountants the next day at my tax conference in Orlando. What a contrast! The writing on the wall was pretty clear from the Auditing partners in the interview, that they didn't really understand or believe in my department's value proposition. In fact after the demise of both Enron and Arthur Andersen, they were more comfortable assigning all the liabilities on us the tax people. It was definitely easier than looking in the mirror. It became apparent that my ideal business model to deliver Personal Financial Services was not from inside an accounting firm run by Audit partners. Despite that bleak foresight into the future, I planned to stay the course through the interview process, but keep my career antennae up. All options open.

~ Consider the Signs when
Life is Directing You Elsewhere ~

PLAY IT BY EAR

~ *Let things Fall as they may,* *and Clarity will come Find You* ~

When I returned home to Atlanta, Keith and I talked everyday. I drove my minivan all over the city, which is surrounded by a beltway. Since all the roads were laid out in this circuitous fashion I referred to locations by the hands of a clock. The girls and I lived around nine o'clock in a little town called Mableton. I could drive directly into the center, Midtown, where my firm's offices were and down to six o'clock pretty easily where my major client, Delta Airlines was headquartered. But beyond that traffic was insane. I couldn't believe that I actually yearned for the congested but organized urban grid of Philadelphia's streets. How was that possible?

We decided we would just play it by ear in determining where and how we would meet. But we would try to meet as often as possible. Keith still traveled a lot since he served as a director on a number of public companies' boards. One of them had acquired an investment advisory firm in Atlanta. He was coming to see me!

At that time Midtown wasn't as developed as
Buckhead and Downtown. Midtown was sandwiched
between them like bookends. Ironically, Keith's
business meetings were nearby, so he booked a room
at The Four Seasons Midtown a few blocks from my
office. Even though he was officially retired, this man
was like a whirling dervish. Yes, I lived out of my
awesome minivan. But it appeared to me that this
man lived out of a plane. He was still jetting around
the country popping up in cities up and down the
eastern seaboard. We planned to meet up on one of
the evenings when my girls were visiting with their
Dad.

 I walked over to meet Keith after work in the hotel's
beautifully appointed Bar Margot. I was still adapting
to the friendly ways of Southern hospitality, where
random patrons actually took time to recognize their
fellow human beings as they imbibed. I was still
adjusting from the hard nosed Northeast where
customers would almost knock each other out to win
an open bar seat. I was starting to really relax in my
own skin, as I grew to appreciate that all the
southern"bless her heart" ways were a much more
pleasant way to live.

Again, upon first glance, I was struck with how
elegantly this man dressed. He clearly loved clothes.
He wore a Navy blue blazer with what looked like a
small gold fleur-de-lis on the left breast pocket, along
with small gold buttons on each cuff. His button

down collared shirt, was a broad, blue windowpane plaid on a subtle pink background. His wool blend trousers were of a soft color that reminded me of carmel, candied apples. My mouth began to water.

Keith had just arrived via taxicab from the Atlanta Hartsfield-Jackson Airport, a seething mass of humanity if there ever was one. His broad Scottish face was alight and smiling as he joked with the bartender. He held up his glass of Macallan 12 on the rocks in a salute, when he saw me enter the expansive space. As he climbed down from his bar stool perch I strode across the room rolling my computer briefcase, aka my global office. By the time I reached him, he had his arms out to embrace me as he gently kissed my mouth, causing me to shiver again at his touch and taste. How I had missed him. Even as I was busy living my single Mom, working career life, there was a corner of my mind occupied with this man and what he was fast becoming to me emotionally.

As we settled back down in a flurry of small talk, I decided to order a Cosmopolitan, which I had now learned was a Cape Cod but fancier with more stuff in it. When asked how I wanted it served, I was now out of data. In a glass? Keith laughed at my cocktail naivete, as he overcame his surprise that there were still adult women that didn't know the difference between a cosmo on the rocks and straight up (without ice in the pretty martini glass that looks like an upside down pyramid).

After watching Keith survive the full frontal (both literal and figurative) feminine wiles of the Palm Beach bar scene, I began to understand how strange I must have appeared to him. I was definitely a conundrum all things considered. Yes I was an adventurous soul as Keith quickly pointed out to me. But that aspect was in stark contrast to my more puritanical church plus straight-laced accounting cross-cultural experiences.

We were definitely having a *Gulliver's Travels* or maybe *Don Quixote* type encounter, where our colliding worlds were often in such contrast. This was made all the more implausible that we were so at home with each other. We were adrift on a sea of two. Through our conversations thus far, we had determined that our physical universes ran parallel but never intersecting until now. We were busy making up for what we saw as lost time.

Perhaps because we were coming from different generations, times and places in our lives, we didn't really want to let anyone else in yet on our secret life. We were quickly building a powerful alliance. I think unconsciously, we knew if we wanted to thrive as a future couple, we needed to hone this synchronicity first.

As a female, I instinctively knew that the "illegitimi" would definitely be out in force trying to find the chinks in our armor to wear us down. Just like the name of Keith's early former employer, Carborundum, funnily named for their grinding wheels and sandpaper. The company was first founded over one hundred and twenty years ago by Acheson. He was a tinkerer scientist that was trying to make diamonds out of carbon. Alchemy really. His failure to do so resulted in a ubiquitous invention that is still a staple of today's world: sandpaper. How symbolic.

I slowly began to flush with pleasure, as Keith told me he had booked a table for two at an up and coming restaurant. But he wanted to surprise me, so he had also reserved a town car through the hotel, to drive us. That was the first of a number of dinners where Rufus was our chauffeur, whisking us through the endless Atlanta traffic. Therefore Rufus was also the first person we let in on our secret. It was such a pleasant luxury to relax and let others be in charge of decisions, itineraries and destinations for once. I hadn't let anyone take care of me in a long time, and it actually felt really good to be valued and coddled.

I still hadn't learned how to slow down and stop barreling through doors at full speed. It would take a bit of re-learning before I could appreciate the gallant sign of respect Keith exhibited by opening doors on dates. But one step at a time.

~ Surprises and the Unexpected
can often Bring great Joy ~

CROSSING THE RUBICON

~Loving Rituals can Build Meaning ~

Rufus dropped us off in front of a newly acclaimed restaurant in Buckhead called JOËL which had its own, strange French pronunciation, joe-ell. It was early enough that the sun was setting through the plate glass windows and a cocktail crowd cluttered the bar. As we sat down for dinner, we naturally sat catty corner to each other, with Keith on my right. The sunbeams from the sinking sun filtered through the table's crystal glasses creating prisms on the tablecloth.

A poem started to form in my head trying to capture this beautiful image:

Catty corner we sat for dinner,
the china chinked and the glasses winked...

I would try to remember this later so I could work on it.

A young woman sommelier came to take care of Keith's wine selection. After her departure, I started to ask Keith about his years at Carborundum. It was where we had left off in our meandering conversations into each others' worlds. We were intent on catching up on decades lived by the other. We even brought our yearbooks and photo albums on visits, so we could understand each other's histories better. We were building constructs of perspective in record time.

Keith's sometimes gruff voice sounded more like a purring relaxed big cat as he began:

"Well, our company's headquarters was located in Niagara Falls about twenty-five miles away from Buffalo, New York. In fact, our CEO Wendel talked Hilton hotels into building a new location across the street. We had people coming from all over the world to see us. Besides Niagara Falls themselves were a big tourist attraction, so the town needed more hotel rooms. Often we would walk across the street and have lunch once it was built. From our offices, you could see the mist rising from the Falls, even though they were a fair walk, maybe a quarter of a mile away from us,"

"Wow, I knew they were powerful, but that's pretty impressive to think about. I woodenya thought it could be that strong," I responded with surprise.

"It was a perfect location for us, because for us to make our two principal products, we required to be near a large water source for cheap electrical power. To make sandpaper, you need both silicon carbide and aluminum oxide, but you needed a huge power source to create the magic. These elements made all kinds of grades of sandpaper and grinding wheels that were used in every kind of business in the world in those days. From car making, construction equipment, manufacturing, everything."

Even though I was never a very big Beatles' fan, I was hearing John Lennon's posthumous refrain echoing, "I'm just sitting here watching the wheels go round and round, I really love to watch them roll." I couldn't help but interject, "So literally you guys made the world go round."

With a corresponding grin, Keith replied, "Yeah, if you can believe it, these were monster size grinding wheels that went on big machines all the way down to little ones that you could buy in a store. This was some really sophisticated stuff in those days and that was principally what we made inside the United States. We also had an environmental group and an insulation group. We made refractory bricks for ovens, and then out of that came refractory insulation material cloth. That was the business that my friend Alex Goldstein started running. We would make this lightweight refractory fiber cloth that went inside of industrial ovens that got up to two or three thousand degrees. That way you didn't have to lay down this heavy brick. People could actually hang this special fiber so it was a much easier installation. Maintenance was a lot easier too, because it was pretty easy to insert a new one instead of tearing out old bricks that had lost their fire retardant nature. It was a huge growth business for a good long while."

As I listened, this magnetic connection continued to burn hotter between us. Pretty soon, my fingers crept under the tablecloth searching for Keith's hand and I placed my fingers through his. I could listen to that sonorous voice forever.

I interjected, "It's so weird, how we all take consumer products like sandpaper for granted. As if they were made out of thin air or grown on a farm or sumpin'. I had no idea it was that complicated to make sandpaper. Touring your old plant would have been a great elementary school field trip, I think."

By this time, Jennifer, the friendly sommelier, brought back the bottle that Keith had picked. Because of his years in South Africa, he had a big soft spot for their wines, and he had found Meerlust hidden in the wine list.

Jennifer and Keith gave me a combined crash course on this ancient vineyard. It was founded in the 1600's in the Stellenbosch region down around Cape Town. They had cabernet sauvignon and pinot noirs. But they also had a famous Bordeaux- like blend named Rubicon. As in crossing the Rubicon like Julius Caesar. As in the awesome Eighties' album, *Frontiers,* by *Journey,* where Steve Perry belts out the words:

"Make a move across the Rubicon, futures knocking at your door… choose the road you want, the opportunity is yours…"

As I lifted the glass of Meerlust to my lips, I could smell its unique aroma, based on its own geographical sourcing. It was changing as it came to life as it met the air. Meditating on these prescient lyrics, I crossed through some doorway. And I didn't want to look back.

As if Keith knew what I was thinking, he said something that resonated, yet it was jarring:

"Erica, I like myself better when I am with you."

It was humbling, because I knew exactly what Keith meant. It was as if I was looking into the mirror that St. Paul referenced where one could only catch a sense. But, I could see my future self, and I liked her a lot more too. She was home.

~ When you Cross your Rubicon,
you become a Better Version of yourself ~

RAMADA INN

~ Pivotal Problems are often Solved
when we struggle Alone in a Silent room ~

We finished our entrees, which were something Frenchy and therefore difficult for me to pronounce. That was what annoyed me the most about fine wine and dining, I had no retention of the illogical enounciations of French words. I had much education on many things, but I successfully avoided foreign languages. I think I was burned out learning the secret language of the U.S. Tax Code, that was brutal enough.

 I left linguistics to my erudite cousin Kyrce, who taught herself random languages for kicks. She learned Korean from binge watching their soap operas on the weekends. That just made my skin crawl thinking about that mental challenge.

So that night, I began the tedious process of building my own phonetically spelled alternative dictionary to help my mind retain this wine lingo. For example, the French Burgundy region Pouilly-Fuisse, I would absolutely butcher. Left to my own devices, I would say something like Pooh-a-illy-phus-ee. I knew better than to trot out my ignorant attempts, so I would just point to the menu item.

 That night I got my head wrapped around that one French word. *Pooh-ee Foo-say*. So everytime I see a wine bottle from Pouilly-Fuisse, my mind has a free association with Winnie the Pooh and the band Kung Fu Fighters. Go figure, but it works.

After dinner, I stirred some honey into a cuppa tea, as the Brits would say. I wanted to know more about Carborundum and how Keith's career choices had led him there. Our conversation turned back to the snowy North, the seventies and Niagara Falls. Keith spoke:

"Well, as we discussed the company needed a power source that was economically efficient to make grinding papers. It would have brought the electrical grid to its knees, and it would have driven the cost of sandpaper to a number that didn't make any economic sense. Therefore, it solved its problem by using a great deal of hydroelectric power."

Joking, I said, "Who wooda thunk it, ya need a water fall to make sand stick to paper!"

Laughing, Keith responded, "Exactly! Niagara Falls doesn't exactly turn off now does it?" with just a hint of amused sarcasm. He continued, "It was a huge power plant, driven by this natural endless power source of running water. Therefore, you don't need to have an energy battery where you store the converted energy, like you do with one of these wind farms today. The water keeps running and you can continuously convert it to electricity. Think on the old water wheels you would see, the wheel would turn, create the energy to grind the grain, a pay as you go system in effect. Falling water in the Norwegian fjords powers all of Norway with cheap hydro-electricity today."

"We then used the energy to electrically charge the crystal structure of alumina and silica, which stunk to high heaven by tha way. We built these special railroad cars open at the top. At the end of each car was either a positive or negative charged graphite electrode. The railcar would be full of the material, once charged its molecular structure changed, and we had the right stuff to make grinding wheels and sandpaper."

Laughing I interjected, "Hence the name Carborundum! Don't let the bastards wear you down! Wow, ain't that the truth," I muttered.

I had yet to see Niagara Falls beyond TV or postcards, but I could imagine what a powerful energy source they would be. Keith's young family was still living down in the Pittsburgh area, when he started his new job in Niagara Falls. For the first month or two Keith rented a room at The Ramada Inn, across the street from the university's basketball arena. During the week, he stayed at the hotel, then he would drive home for the weekends, while starting the arduous process of relocation. While staying at the Ramada, Keith started to delve into the first difficult problem he was assigned by his new employer.

"It was so cold in New York, the wind would come off the lake, it was just brutal particularly cuz I was a South Carolinian. I-ahh remember being holed up in my hotel room working on this complicated Brazilian currency exchange at night. Sometimes, I would take a mental break and scurry across the street to see Niagara University's basketball team play. You may remember the name, Calvin Murphy. At the time he was the country's leading collegiate basketball scorer. He could entertain the crowds. He was sumpin' else. I call it an arena, but it was really this bandbox of a gym that looked more like a quonset hut. When Murphy was running up and down the court, that place was rocking."

I asked, "What was the currency exchange problem?"

"Well, you have to remember this was around 1975, there wasn't as much specific guidance on such esoteric issues from the Financial Accounting Standards Board (FASB). Today there are all sorts of Generally Accepted Accounting Principles (GAAP) on how a company should report the impact of foreign currency valuations on their public financial statements. But back then, we had to figure some of this stuff out on our own. There wuz no guidance."

As the tax CPA, I knew the downright accuracy of his statement. The FASBs that were issued around foreign currency issues started falling fast and furiously off the conveyor belt as we entered the 1990's. From what I recall, it took about ten years for the regulators to catch up on what went down through the eighties between the industrialists and the financial "wizards of Wall Street" who worked every penny of profit from esoteric concepts such as international straddles, mark to market, passive foreign investment corporations and such.

Keith paused to collect his thoughts for a moment, as he took off his collegiate gold signet ring from his finger and started spinning it on the crisp white table cloth. You could see his mind was far away in that lonely room trying to forge a new path.

"I had to figure it out for myself. I was hired as Assistant Treasurer and reported to Paul Meyer. Paul asked me to try to tackle this problem, because I had more experience in this specialized area already than he did. I did this kinda stuff when I started a Dupont. In fact, I wrote a memo about that, but that's a different story for a another night. Then Ahh had spent a lotta time in Brazil when I was working for a firm in Pittsburgh."

"What firm was that?" I asked, curiously.

"It's a firm Ahh would like to forget. The only thing I learned there was patience. At least that is what I would always say," Keith quipped. Yet he bravely continued on:

"You know those old green fourteen and twenty-one column legal size accounting workpapers? So I was setting up these side by side worksheets. One set was Carborundum's consolidated balance sheet without the Brazilian company. Then one consolidation including the subsidiary with the Brazilian cruzeiros translated into U.S. dollars. Then I would work out the inter-company transfers, which as you know ensures you don't double count sh*t. Back then the FASB hadn't issued any regulatory guidance, so we had to figure out a reasonable method to report the financial impact ourselves. As a public company, we were required to report a fair set of financials to the world."

I noted, living inside a public accounting firm, I knew how far the industry did progress since these earlier days of more primitive accounting. I couldn't help but interject, "Well, we don't have that problem anymore. Bibles of accounting standards have been written since then. But regardless, if people choose to commit fraud, regulations are not gonna stop anybody."

With that, we had had enough of rules, regulations and what would constitute a qualified opinion. Words were suddenly quite meaningless, and there was really nothing left to be said.

~ No matter the quantity of Regulation,
Frauds have a Direct reciprocal Relationship
with the Lack of Moral Fiber ~

WITH THE GIRLS

~ *Something Furry is sometimes the best Medicine* ~

I was still walking around three feet off the ground after that last dinner. I was thinking about how the sands of time had run out on us again. Keith and I had to part ways and go back into our busy lives. I was enjoying the feeling of looking forward to the next time and place, when we were together again wherever that might be.

I was back at home, well at the brand new Atlanta house. My new chapter in life as a single Mom, in a new city, charging for a new promotion, had a lot of wrinkles smoothed out when Lizzie appeared.. Like a modern day Mary Poppins, Lizzie fit right in; she was the spoonful of sugar herself! According to the agency, we would try each other out for a week on a trial basis. But it was like a knife through butter from that very first day. When it was time for her to leave on the very first trial day, my youngest, Chloe, wrapped her little four-year old arms around Liz' leg at departure time, "No Lizzie, please don't goooo." And from that first night, a silly but important ritual began.

As Liz pulled her car into the cul-de- sac, to leave, Chloe and eight-year-old Hannah "chased her up the hill" on foot, running parallel in the sidewalk.

Walking with children through a divorce is never an easy thing. Often one feels like the proverbial candle in the wind that Elton John wrote and sang about it, others' opinions of what you should do overriding you. When I look back to my Amazon history of orders (isn't it weird that they are still out there?), I had ordered a bunch of books about how to help children be more comfortable going between two parents' homes. It was complicated. If you try to think about this recurring transition as a four or eight year old, you can see how frustrating the process could be. Thankfully, they didn't have to hop on a plane to go visit Dad, like some kids did, it was a half hour car ride.

One of the ways, I felt that would help the girls adjust to their newly acquired dual-home status was if each girl could get a cat. So one day, after we "chased Lizzie up the hill" as part of our goodbye routine, I was flipping through the mail. It was as if the angels heard my thoughts, for there was a postcard from the local veterinarian advertising two sister kittens in need of a new home. I gave them a call on the spot, and before we knew it, the three of us were at the vets' peering through the bars of a pet kennel at two kittens!

Hannah, blessed with a boundless source of inner energy, bounced with joy as the employee opened the cage's door. Her light brown hair was flying out behind her in all directions, with each bounce, as she moved at the speed of light. Her honey brown eyes danced with excitement, as she thrust her flying hands into the cage trying to pick up her new cat, any cat! Little sister, Chloe, was behind her shoulder peering up, through even darker chocolate bangs, trying to catch a glimpse too.

At first, Hannah grasped for the smoke-gray tortoise cat, who deftly avoided her hands and scooted into the back corner of the cage, unwilling to be subdued by human touch. And as if it was meant to be, her tabby-striped sister came forward, and stood still, which allowed Hannah to enfold her furry kitten-body, oh so close to Hannah's own heart. It was as if the sister cats knew that Hannah was going to need more of a lap cat variety. Hannah quickly named her more docile pet, Samantha, who seemed quite up to the task of being smothered and twisted into interesting pretzel shapes.

Solemnly, four year old Chloe stepped forward to meet her kitten. With that unfathomable dark chocolate gaze, she stared into the touchier cat's green eyes in what I feared would become a Mexican stand-off. Secretly I groaned, picturing images of Hannah bonded with her cat for life, and Chloe did not, another sibling rivalry to referee. But slowly, Chloe extended her chubby right index finger into the cage. The smoky-gray came closer to the extended "olive branch" and rubbed her full flank down her finger. A successful sisterly detente, both feline and humane.

~When you think you Know
what's Best for others,
Reconsider Intervention and Let things Unfold ~

ACCELERATION CAN BE EXHILARATING

~ Keep close those who Motivate You
to be a Better version of Yourself ~

When we planned our next adventure, it was after a rather unexpected arrival for Keith. He was outrunning a Floridian hurricane. We met inside Buckhead's high-falutin, splendid Lumen bar at the Ritz-Carlton. Dark mahogany wood wainscoting, crystal chandeliers, upscale Southern charm oozing from the comfy couches.

But the best part of this metropolitan setting was the live music. Tonight it was a trio, an alto crooning lyrics, while she was backed up by a strumming guitarist and pianist.

I was wound up, like a caged leopard that had finally been released back into the wild. I had spent the day holed up in my shared office in lock down trying to jam out CPE also known as Continuing Professional Education credits to keep my CPA license active and in good standing.

According to my original state licensure, I had to have eighty hours of qualified credits, every two years. Eight had to be Tax, sixteen in Audit or Accounting, four in Ethics, and a minimum of twenty hours annually. Needless to say, I had to keep a rolling spreadsheet to make sure that I could tick off all of the boxes when my state's board decided to audit me, which seemed to happen every period.

As a tax accountant at a Final Four public accounting firm, I spent countless hours in internal meetings that would qualify as CPE, so I normally had hundreds of overall qualified hours, way beyond the required eighty. But I would be missing the elusive Audit and Accounting credits, since I was a full time tax specialist.

Therefore, when other people were getting ready for New Year's Eve, I would often be in a mad online scramble trying to get the last two darn hours of Audit and Accounting credits, to make the sixteen required hours for that reporting period. So today, I was feeling quite smug with myself, here it was September, I was four months ahead of schedule! I completed my annoying quest! I found some on Fraud topics, at least I had an interest in that. And I was done! Definitely a reason to celebrate my surprise alacrity as opposed to procrastination with Keith who had just rolled into town.

"I just needed the right kind of motivation to get that box checked," I muttered to myself as my face lit up when I saw my Braveheart across a crowded room one more time.

~ Who inspires you to excel and accelerate? ~

CRIMES OF OPPORTUNITY

~ *Sometimes Seeing for Oneself* *is the Best of all Teachers* ~

Keith was fresh from his surprise road trip due to Hurricane Ivan, spinning in circles over the entire state of Florida. He was in a full state of high spirit, his Scottish skin flushed a light pink, as he regaled the bartender with stories of his own collegiate days tending the bar at Lake George.

As I strode up to the bar, in my Jones New York all business burgundy pants suit, I was so happy to see the man in my life, I was grinning ear to ear. As Keith rose to greet me in that second-natured way that Southern gentleman appear to own in spades, I grabbed his two cheeks between my hands and kissed him on the mouth, which definitely surprised this man-in-charge.

"I am so glad that you are SAFE after that long road trip all by yourself!" I exclaimed. Continuing in a more joking tone after my dramatic public attack, "I can't believe you drove through a hurricane to come and see me. I am quite beguiled by this gallantry," I quipped.

As I settled down by Keith's side, we began shooting the breeze like most people do by talking about the weather. Violent patterns were rocking the South in the summer of 2004. Not only was Ivan still roaring, Hurricane Jeanne was busy kicking up the Atlantic; apparently she was going to ride Ivan's coattails right into the East coast of Florida too.

Keith's vibrating baritone boomed, "Iahhh swear, haffa Palm Beach checked into the Ritz with me. I've seen more Palm Beachers here in the executive floor lounge than I've seen living on my own street the past few months! And Ahmm not going back until this thang blows itself out. Yah can't screw around with hurricanes cuz they will tear you up! Ahm a belts and suspenders kinda guy, I don't mess around."

As Keith broke down all of the hurricane proofing steps he completed with the fastidious help of Charles, his property manager, it sounded like a Fort Knox type solution. What else could you do but prepare and get out of the way?

We ordered appetizers from the bartender, some shrimp cocktail and crab cakes. We moved into what I had so proudly accomplished that day, the completion of my Fraud accounting credits. I began:

"I think I picked frauds today to study, because they are a comment on the human condition. What I learned confirmed what I already felt. Most financial frauds that are discovered are committed by first time offenders. They are crimes of opportunity. Nine out of ten people caught in a financial fraud had never been caught in any other type of crime. So what does this mean right? It means that yah can't really legislate or regulate against fraud. You can't really weed out theft by WHO you hire. We have to recognize that pretty much ANYONE when presented with an opportunity to get away with a financial theft, will attempt to commit it. It is human nature."

Keith interrupted, "Well that's kinda *hawd* to believe. But let me think about *thah* for a minute."

I was getting riled up and kept barreling on, "Just think about it. As managers in a business we have to keep our eyes and ears open. If it doesn't smell right or look right, it probably isn't. Frauds are crimes of opportunity. Does it look like the person's circumstances have changed? Based on this study, nine out of ten financial frauds are committed because the person believes that they will NOT get caught. They didn't plan it, the opportunity just presented itself and they took the bait. That's a lot harder to regulate against, you have to change your underlying presumption as an employer, that anyone is susceptible and focus more on preventing opportunities. If you tempt most people with a honeypot, they will bite."

Then Keith said, "Well, I tell you what, you might be onto something here. I do have a case I dealt with

about a fraud I discovered when I was CEO at
Hercules. This was in the 1990's. I had spent a
weekend reviewing the entire company's performance
for the quarter. Something wasn't adding up in one of
our eight divisions."

"I wasn't sure if I was right, but it smelled like a fraud,
but I couldn't prove it yet. So, I decided to do my own
analysis based on my own perception. Then I took
the necessary steps to secretly investigate it to prove
my own analysis before making accusations or
involving others. If I was proven right, there were big
consequences for it."

*~ Come at a Problem from Different Angles and
Question Everything to Identify the Cause ~*

APPLICATIONS OF INVENTIONS CAN BIRTH WHOLE INDUSTRIES

~ One Invention can have many Applications ~

"Wow, that sounds really intense. What happened?" I asked curiously.   I was fiddling around with my cocktail napkin, trying to dab my lips without losing all of my lipstick all at once on its surface.

"Well, we had a division called the fibers division which made polypropylene fiber for multiple uses, but the largest application by far was disposable diapers.

I asked, "Wait. Isn't polypropylene a type of plastic made from oil? Is that what diapers are made out of? Diapers are made out of an oil based product?" I was thinking of all the diapers I had changed as a young mother. The fact that disposable diapers were an oil-based product just seemed so oxymoronic.

With that sphinx-like smile, Keith continued, "Well in our case yes. But scientists can actually make polypropylene out of a bunch of different kinda feedstocks ranging from plant based (such as sugar cane) to non-renewable sources such as fuel-based products, like natural gas or naphtha. But ironically, just cuz a plastic is made from a plant-based source does NOT mean it is biodegradable."

In response I added, "I just read somewhere, sumpin about ethanol, the corn-based additive in gasoline. How ethanol ends up driving up the cost of corn in other end products, so there can be unexpected consequences."

As I tried to imagine the complex reconfiguring of fuel molecules into a cloth fiber, I took another sip of this sparkling Italian wine that was much calmer than the bubbly Champagnes from France. Something new again on my rookie palate. The combination of a new taste on my tongue and new intellectual concepts gliding down my auditory canals carried a powerful dual-sensory punch. I was getting intoxicated, and it was not from the few sips of wine I just had. It was from the knowledge and energy pumping out of this man.

Keith was moving into the revenue end of diapers now, "Our largest customer by far was Procter & Gamble who made Pampers and Luvs. But we also had the other major producer, Kimberly-Clark as a customer too. They made the Huggies brand."

"Well, as a Mom, I hafta add my two cents here, and say Pampers was the best. I hated Huggies. I liked that Pampers had the plastic exterior shell instead of just the cloth-like material throughout. It seemed like the urine would seep through and it would become damp."

With a look of surprise, Keith said, "Really? Well somehow one of our sales guys convinced P&G to buy this additional specialized film to put on the outside of their product."

"Well whoever that was, was right, cuz it worked." After a pause, I added, "It is kinda mind boggling thinking about how many people and inventions can be involved keeping a baby's bottom clean," I ended with a light laugh.

"Yeah, we actually made two kinds of polypropylene fibers that went in-tah a diaper, hydrophilic and hydrophobic."

Musing, I interrupted, "Well I know from my high school Greek independent study class that hydro is water. Philic is derived from phileo which is love and phobic is fear, so the philic would absorb..."

Keith completed my sentence, "...the insult, so it was placed in the center of the diaper. Then the hydrophobic was placed around the leg openings of the diaper so it would shun the insult and force it to flow towards the super absorbent in the center."

"That is crazy, how much tweaking of formulas and application that went into a quote simple diaper! But we haven't gotten to the fraud part yet, I want to hear about how you discovered the fiber fraud."

But at that moment, a hostess came to seat us at a table for dinner. So the Fiber Fraud Story was going to have to wait. As we climbed down from our bar stool perches, my eyes rested on Keith's broad back and shoulders wrapped in a navy blazer. There was pixie dust in the air again. Yes, some secret formula was brewing between us. I couldn't break down its components yet. But I could only classify our brewing formula as magical.

~ *When you work to Perfect Formulas, one day you may find Magic. When you do, Take Time to Discover the many new Applications* ~

THE FIBER FRAUD

~ Often the most Important Aspect of any Discovery is Following your niggling Instinct to its Source ~

As Christine cleared our first course of butternut squash soup, made with coconut milk, we began to relax. The anxieties of homesteads being destroyed by Hurricane Ivan and tax deadlines were temporarily shelved. As we spun stories, there was a palpable ache in my heart, that Keith was so far away from me on the other side of this cozy corner in the back of the Lumen bar. I couldn't quite reach his hand across the broad table, I hadn't seen him for a couple weeks, and it had been long enough.

At his core, I knew Keith was a much more formal personality than me. After all, he had been raised in the South by Sarah Belle Broome, who used a fork as a cattle prod if Keith forgot his manners at the table. On the other hand, my Mother's lessons were often ploughed over by my Pop's complete disregard of etiquette. His interaction with humanity trumped all these less important details. Besides his informality, Pop loved to call himself Pastor Chevy Chase, as in the movie Family Vacation. This was due to the fact that in his zeal for life, he could be a complete klutz and evoke disasters such as accidentally setting the yard on fire doing routine landscaping chores. Clearly, Keith and I were coming from two different ends of the genetic spectrum.

But regardless, if I could figure out a way to surreptitiously touch him while we were separated by this table, I could really relax and settle in. With that I slouched down into my banquette, upholstered seat and kicked off my heels. I stretched my long legs under the table, shrouded in white linen, until I could rest one socked foot on the outside of each of Keith's muscled thighs. No one could see, right? Why shouldn't I? Even so I could see that Scottish pink flush creeping up from his color to Keith's hairline. So funny! Keith could barnstorm the world of business and not flinch. But the ghost of Sarah Belle could terrorize him from the grave.

I murmured my own prayer to Sarah Belle reminding her that her only son had been lonely for a long time and I was here to love him. Outwardly, I jabbed:

"Whuh? No one can see! I need to touch you, while you tell me the Fiber Fraud story!" Besides it was funny to finally find something that was outside Keith's comfort zone. Turn-about is fair play.

Keith collected himself, when he realized my feet weren't gonna move. I could see him gathering his thoughts, placing them in order under his hooded eyelids. He was such a good story teller, it came naturally to him. Again, I recalled how I wanted to capture them all on paper, there was so much value here that would disappear into the ether if they weren't written down. Our modern culture had lost the art of oral storytelling. To save personal histories, they needed to be down in print. (So years later, here we are, finally!) Keith began:

"We had a financial reporting system that put out a book each month on each of our businesses. It was basically an internal report card, this was before company emails and PDF attachments, so it was a printed book. We had eight major businesses, that Gossage christened franchises, to show how discreet they were from one another. Each business' book was not that thick, as they did not get down into the weeds. They were prepared for me as a top side summary in my role as Chief Executive."

"We also printed more detailed books for each Franchise's General Manager so they could review the depths of what was going on in their own businesses. But for the financial function and the senior officers of the company we used this monthly summary so we could perform more useful forward thinking analysis. Normally, I would take one afternoon each month, and review the material, usually from two to six thirty or seven p.m. Then I would take it home and review some more for about another one and a half to two hours. By the next morning, I felt like I was completely up to date for each business."

I murmured, "When I study for something, it always seemed important to sleep on the material. Somehow it felt like it became embedded while I was unconscious. I knew it better the next day then the day I studied it."

Unperturbed, Keith continued, "So after about three months, the fiber division's numbers just looked strange to me. In all the kind of measurements that I thought were important something just didn't smell right on that franchise's reports. Apparently, the plant was running flat out at a non-stop rate. Ironically, our major fiber plant was in a small town right here outside of Atlanta. What was the name of that place? I'll think of it in a minute...Anyways, this was August, September and October. In November, I became pretty suspicious because the performance numbers had really cranked up, and it was the Fall, and we were heading towards our annual results. These determined the bonus levels across the company for everybody. Therefore, the general manager of each division, the division controller, the plant's manager and controller, everybody in that division, in effect would benefit. The definition of collusion."

"LaGrange, Georgia! That was it! Why couldn't I remember that? I musta repressed it!

Now that expression got me busting out laughing so hard, that wine started coming out through my nose, which was NOT a pretty picture whatsoever! As I struggled to breathe, Keith was still barreling onward telling truths:

"Anyways, I was reading public earnings reports from Procter & Gamble and Kimberly-Clark. Both companies commented at the end of their second and third quarters that their diaper sales were depressed. And cuz uh that, the big dip in sales of their most profitable item was a direct hit to their bottom line. The loss in sales was a profit killer."

As Keith got closer to the exposure of the fraud's mechanics, his vocal tenor got more resonant and emphatic:

"So, if their businesses were off from their plans, it should also have been a direct hit on our fiber plant's own productivity and subsequent earnings. And yet our plant, which supplied 100% of Procter & Gamble's diaper fiber and 40% of Kimberly-Clark's, was still running completely flat out"

"The part that was the most troubling was, it wasn't just an increase in inventory. Since our customers weren't buying, all that extra fiber should-a been sitting in our inventory, but it wuzz-int. Instead, we were reporting really strong divisional sales numbers, even though simultaneously our two biggest customers' sales numbers were down. When you looked at it from thirty thousand feet, it just didn't make any sense."

At that point, our friendly server, Christine appeared with our main courses. I was trying something new for me, it was a stewed kind of rabbit dish, which was really quite delicious. Keith was having lamb chops with this interesting side of roasted root vegetables. As I enjoyed the delicious flavors and the gamey smells wafting from my plate, I paused to look at this powerhouse of a man sitting across from me. He was something else. His brain power was downright intoxicating by itself. I settled in a bit more as I continued to listen. I liked how he thought for himself. It resonated with my personal philosophy to trust no one else to form my personal opinions.

"The plant was running three full shifts, twenty-four hours a day." With a nod of recognition Keith said, "Now for somebody that understands accounting you can run a plant absolutely flat out and you know that what it does is absorb all the fixed costs of keeping the plant open. I was suspicious they were pulling this stunt, which is a typical accounting trick. But this seemed bigger than that, when I thought about our customers' financial reporting."

Thinking it through out loud, I complained, "Well, I do remember first off how much I HATED my cost accounting course. It was so dry! All these formulas Fixed Costs (FC) + Variable Costs (VC) equals your Total Costs (TC) blah blah blah. But, yes, I understand that the Fixed Costs don't move, regardless. If it costs a million dollars a year to keep your operating plant open before you make your first unit of product that is your Fixed Cost (FC). If you decide not to make any products for one year, you still have to pay the fixed costs like real estate taxes, mortgage, insurance, and utilities. Some entrepreneurs call it "The Carry", I paused to take a small sip of wine then continued.

"So, when you finally make your very first unit of product for sale, you begin to apply the pro rata share of the FC across all units produced. So the more you can run your plant, the smaller the percentage of your fixed costs are for each of your "widgets" or whatever it is that you are making. Of course the rub is, you better be able to sell them all."

It was much more fun thinking about cost accounting theory as it applied to a real life problem. As I tried to figure out the fraud for myself I asked curiously, "But what were they going to do with all this excess fiber? If they were just running the plant flat out twenty-four seven, they would have all of this inventory flowing through their cost of goods sold. Whether it was raw materials, work in progress or finished goods it would be in their Ending Inventory (EI), right?"

My eyes rolled back into my head as I tried to visualize the inventory's effect on the income statement. I continued to mutter, "...But EI is subtracted AWAY from ending Cost of Goods Sold (COGS), so it would make COGS smaller, so that would actually INCREASE their profit on their income statement...And they would have all of this massive inventory reported, increasing their assets on the balance sheet..so how was this gonna benefit them in their personal pocketbooks?"

Keith picked up my thread of thought "Yes so that is where it was really bad, the crux of the fraud. They didn't have anyone to sell it to since the diaper-making customers had all stopped their regular orders! I spent a lotta mah time designing compensation plans for company employees to drive the behavior we needed to achieve company results. And I sure as sh*t didn't intend to design a comp plan to pump out a whole lotta inventory that nobody wanted to buy!"

Puzzled, I asked, "So what did they think they were gonna do with it? How did they plan to turn it into a bonus-able event?" As my curiosity stirred the pot, I continued, "That's what happens with fraudsters! You have to keep up the pretense, you have to perpetrate another fraud to cover up the previous fraud! One fraud begets the next!"

I thought to myself, how did he stay so calm talking about this? I was wound up now listening to him spin this tale albeit years later!

Nodding his head in agreement, Keith explained, "I got suspicious when I reviewed their monthly income statement and balance sheet. Something just didn't smell right. I was guessing that they were making up FAKE sales on the income statement and then big fake receivables on the balance sheet. But I didn't really know, I was guessing. I didn't wanna accuse anybody inside the company yet, without making some more independent verifications."

Interrupting, I chimed in, "To quote your friend Walt Mahler, 'Do ya wanna make a decision with more or less data?' Right?"

"Exactly," Keith continued. "If I was right that they had faked sales, that was where simple mismanagement crossed the line to big time fraud. As a public company, if the fraud had grown unchecked, we coulda been in really big trouble. We coulda had a material weakness in the external auditors' opinion of our financial statements and that wooda been death. But before I went accusing anybody, and risking a possible large scale internal cover up, I was going to talk to mah friend, John Pepper over at P&G."

By this time, Keith was so intent in his story, he had taken off his gold signet college ring again to spin it on the tablecloth between his burly fingers. It appeared to be a memory jogger for him. His eyes had turned into crescent moon slits, as his mind turned towards the past as he recounted his next steps.

"So I called up Pepper. Ahh really liked him, we came into our CEO roles around the same time. He sat in Cincinnati, where Procter & Gamble was headquartered."

Suddenly, I recalled the visual image that Keith had described to me previously. His plastic green folder that he carried with him at all times. He kept a laminated copy of his Top Priorities List stapled to the front of this folder. It included things such as "visit top ten customers each year". The CEO for P&G would definitely be one of them.

"Ahh remember the first time I met him, I went to see him at his offices, since he was one of our important customers. Ahh took Harry Tucci with me, he was our head of development at the time. When Harry found out I was going out there thah first time, he said to me, 'I think I went to school with their CEO,' When Linda set up my initial visit the message came back, 'Make sure you bring Harry!' And that was that! Anyways, when it came to my suspicions about the fraud, I felt like I knew thah man enough to divulge my fear and see if John could help me gather more data."

By this time I sat enrapt in silence as I listened to Keith spin this tale of fraudulent fiber detection. The loneliness was palpable. I had this picture in my mind's eye, Keith sitting in his beautiful CEO office overlooking the Brandywine River in the heart of Wilmington, Delaware. I could see him at his desk late at night pouring over reports, utterly alone. I could see Norman Rockwell's pictorialized Cop peering down from his *Runaway* painting, which hung behind Keith's mahogany desk. This artistic rendering was the only sentry keeping watch with Keith that night, as he considered the few options available to him. Perpetually spinning his ring across his wooden desk, when he decided to reach outside the walls of his own company, to find out if he had a betrayal within.

~ External Verification can be Vital to document Internal Intuition ~

WHEN SUMS DON'T ADD UP

~ *Often Verification means going to the Point of Conflict Yourself* ~

By this time, Christine quietly cleared our plates, and brought me a cup of coffee. We still were sipping on Keith's red wine selection from dinner too.

I said, "I can't imagine how lonely and angry you must have felt all at the same time. I could see if you asked a question like that inside the company, it would spread like wildfire. It would take a whole two seconds for the perpetrator, or more likely the group, to be notified. They would be covering their tracks like mad and…"

Growling, Keith agreed, "Yes, I was suspicious that if I was right, the fraud had begun at the top of this profitable division. Its General Manager was extremely well known in the Wilmington community, where our headquarters were located. He was president of a local country club. I didn't want to set off alarm bells and give him the chance to cover it up. And I definitely didn't want to wrongly accuse him either! So I got John Pepper on the phone and asked if he could verify his recent invoices with us. He asked for a half hour to contact his Vice President in charge of the diapers division which bought our fiber product. I asked for confidentiality. When I got the return call from the VP, it was as I predicted. He verified that they had definitely slowed down their orders from us for at least a few quarters, and therefore I should expect to see a slow down of production at our corresponding plant."

"Wow, what a punch in the gut," was about all I could muster, imagining how infuriating it must have felt to be informed by your customer of an employee's internal fraud!

 With a nod of his head, Keith continued, "So obviously it was important to keep this information to myself until I could get down to the Georgia based operations. I wanted to see the location of the fraud with my own eyes before I confronted the executive who sat down the hall from me, who was most likely the one who put this accounting fraud into play. I wanted to ferret out myself, at exactly what level the fraud had started. To quote Shakespeare, more often than not the fish stinks from the head, and the head sat a mere few doors down the hall from me. Before I looked him in the eyes, I wanted to know everything."

By this time, I had edged around the corner of the upholstered banquette, so I could plant my chilly toes more firmly under Keith's right thigh. I slide further down the back of the couch, until my neck rested against the back cushion. Keith's mind was focused on his storyline. So it was unconsciously that Keith wrapped his right hand around my foot, and squeezed it each time he emphasized an important point. This was a sign to me. Normally, I couldn't bear anyone touching my feet; they were so ticklish. But here I was in a public restaurant, with Keith's hand wrapped around my foot, and I was completely relaxed. The world must be ending, well at least my world was ending as I knew it!

His voice plowed onward along this lonely path of painful discovery:

"I wanted to arrive at the plant completely unannounced, so none of the players in the fraud had a chance to work on a cover up. So one morning, I called our flight center which was located at our company's hangar at the New Castle County Airport. I told them to file a flight plan to New York City for 7 a.m. and get the plane ready to go. When I arrived at our hangar, all was set, so I boarded and we took off. But about twenty minutes into our flight, I walked up to the flight deck to speak with our two company pilots. I told them, we were changing our plan to this particular airfield in a small town in Georgia. I warned them they weren't authorized to contact anyone in the Hercules organization, about the change in our destination. It would be a fireable offense. In case there was a mishap, I had already told Linda, my executive assistant, of my expected change in travel plans. She had my total confidence at all times. She never violated it."

"Did you tell Linda what was afoot?" I asked curiously.

"I know I didn't tell her the details of my suspicion, but I said something like I had some serious concerns, and if I was right, it would be like bagging a few rats!"

"Now that is a Southern expression I have not heard!" I couldn't believe how many figurative, unusual ways they had to say something. I mused to myself that one day I was going to get to the source of this regional linguistic mystery.

"Normally, Linda would have a car ordered and waiting for me on planned arrivals. But not this time! When I arrived at the small airfield, I took a taxi to remain anonymous as long as possible and maintain the element of surprise. As we made our twenty-five minute drive to the plant, the driver was real talkative. He asked why I was going to the plant."

I interjected, "Ahh another external verifiable source. The most important data can come from the most unexpected places."

Nodding his head, Keith continued:

"When I explained that I was the CEO, the cabbie asked, 'Why aren't you in a fancy car?' Then amazingly, he began to open up: 'Well you guys have got to be doing a fabulous business at this plant!' When I asked why he said, 'Cuz, every warehouse in five miles of it is chock full of fiber. Mah cuzzin in the real estate business happened to mention to me that they are looking for more warehouse space to lease.' Well then I had another confirmation of what my tummy had been telling me all along," Keith paused reliving the painful emotions of that moment.

I interjected, "It takes a lot of nerve to just ask the simple question why. It can stop all the clocks."

Strangely, it was the one word that my four year old already knew how to use. And she did stop time with that argumentative monosyllabic response!

But at that point Christine returned bearing our check. When we looked around the restaurant, we realized we had closed it down again. Apologetically, she told us her shift was over and we could settle up with the bartender if we wanted to stay longer. Keith wanted her to be able to cash out with her own tips for the night. So we paused the storytelling so Keith could settle our debts.

~ Often Verification of your Original thoughts comes from Unexpected Sources ~

CONFRONTATION

~ One can feel at Home in new Circumstances for different Reasons ~

We left the dining room and moved back into the bar area, which now contained an entirely different crowd. This bar appeared to attract a number of younger adult locals looking for nightlife opportunities. Lots of tall women like myself, all comfortable in their long-skins, wearing heels with proud elegant postures.

 One of the things I noticed since my move to Atlanta was the difference in average height of its citizens. To this point, I had lived my entire life as a resident of the Greater Philadelphia area. In my bare feet, I stood five foot eleven inches. Back in Philly, most women were a LOT shorter than me. There were huge neighborhoods of Italian, Jewish and Irish backgrounds surrounding my random, personal homes over the years.. Many (not all) of these women were very petite, relative to me. I towered over all of my friends back in Philly. But here in Atlanta, there were many, many women that I looked right in the eye. I didn't feel like such a gangly giant here. Different place, different reasons to feel at home. And with

Keith everything was different, and I was more at home with this man than with anyone else in my entire life. How could I feel this way, so quickly? As I mused, I could hear Keith working up to the point of confrontation at the place of the fraud.

Keith growled, "I walked in and the people at the front desk had no idea who I was, so I asked if I could see the plant manager and the controller for the plant. After the receptionist called the plant manager's officer, she asked for my name so she could relay who was asking for the two people with the most responsibility at that location. I only gave her my name, Keith Elliott, not my title, and the next thing I heard her say over the phone was, 'Hello? Hello?' Suddenly, the plant manager came tearing around the corner like he was in a hot trot."

My sides started shaking with laughter at this point. I imagined the look on that man's face as he approached Keith. It must have been a look of combined shock and terror of being caught out. Seeing Keith standing there in one of his double-breasted Saville Row suits with french cuffs and a pink tie. Mmmm. Giggling, I pointed out:

"I'm amazed the man didn't have a stroke, he must have thought he was looking into the eyes of the grim reaper." But Keith appeared to have regressed into a sort of trance reliving the actual event; he continued with his eyes closed into slits, and his hands calmly folded on the bar top.

Keith was wearing an almost priest-like mask, as he unfolded the following dialogue that took on the feel of a confessional:

"The man's voice was nervous and shaking. He wanted to know what I was doing there. When I told him I wanted to see for myself how things were going, he seemed to turn a shade paler. When I said a conference room was probably better, and we needed the plant's controller to attend to, the blood drained straight from his face."

"We sat down at the long oblong table, so the three of us sat down around one corner. I summed up my investigation for the two plant's leaders, informing them of my suspicions, investigation of their division's financial statements, and comparison to Procter & Gamble and Kimberly-Clark's earnings releases. I detailed the conversations I had with these important customers to confirm that their diaper businesses were indeed in decline. Then I got into the weeds regarding my dark suspicions about their inventory numbers, and my desire to come and see for myself. When I got to the cab driver's chummy conversation about all the fluffy fiber stuffed into every commercial crevice along the way, you could see their hearts stop. They started stammering and confirmed all of it."

"So I asked again, 'But your inventory numbers don't show that kind of level of unsold inventory at ALL! So what is going on here?' They were stupefied and just kinda sat there."

"I will tell you what I think is going on! I think that you've been told to run the plant flat out so you can absorb the fixed cost of overhead, then your income statement will look good for the year. Of course, you will earn your normal or better bonus. But here is the problem, somehow you now have to now figure out what to do with all that excess inventory before it's discovered!"

Keith paused to collect his thoughts after reliving the intensity of that exchange. I was transfixed. I had heard a lot of fraud discovery stories, but never one recounted in this singular, fiery fashion. The typical solution would only come in a tribunal formation after hours of tortured ringing of the hands in an HR office with lots of attorneys opining on what we could and couldn't say.

This man was the bravest, who else would have the b*lls to take this singular course of action? No one actually. People psychologically avoid uncovering a hornet's nest, because it is too painful. Even less are willing to take on the nest alone, they need a legion of support. It's like sawing off your leg in a last ditch effort of survival.

Unbidden a singular thought rolled off my tongue, now that we were into hardcore truth telling, "I wish I was there. I wish I had been there, so you wouldn't have had to do this so very alone." I placed my hand over Keith's clasped hands in a helpless gesture of sympathy, too little and definitely, way too late.

Keith painfully but simply continued, "So I asked about the lying on the financial entries to hide the fact of the excess physical inventory, literally stuffing the local warehouses chock full. Clearly the numbers didn't reflect the actual fiber strewn about the county. Our company inventory that they had churned out wasn't even on the books. It was downright theft, because you have a company asset no longer accounted for in the financials! That's when I told them what we were going to do. We were getting on the speaker phone with their Direct Reports back up in our Delaware Headquarters: their Fiber Division's General Manager and Controller. We would get the Internal Auditor on the phone too, to figure out what to do next, painful as that was!"

I couldn't imagine how painful that must have been. Forget the sawing off the leg analogy. It must have felt more like harakiri, the Japanese method of suicide by self-induced disembowelment. As I felt the pain in my own guts of this betrayal, I heard Keith's growl continuing on this painful journey:

"And another thing! When I asked the secretary to conference us in on the speaker phone, I walked out and told her to hold everything. I double checked that she had hung up the line at her desk. I told her we were having a very confidential meeting, and if she tried to listen in she wouldn't have a job after that day and her mouth about hit the floor."

As my own jaw dangled, I could definitely imagine how hers had too! Keith's bulldog determination was a mind-blower. Just listening to this insane story of grand larceny and corporate fraudulent intrigue to the tune of millions of dollars was making my adrenaline pump ten or fifteen years later.

When I looked down on the beautiful granite countertop, my hands were balled into clenched fists and the tendons in my neck felt like they were going to pop out of my throat. I looked over to Keith's brawny hands, tranquilly clasped in this relaxed prayerful fold, like a cherubic choir boy at confession. But when I turned to look directly into Keith's eyes, they were as old as the granite underneath our hands' palms. It was as if they had already seen all that could possibly go wrong in the world of humanity, nothing would surprise him anymore.

And at least in this fraud case, he knew the safest way back to sanity, was to scale the dark abyss alone and find the bottom before he unleashed the solution, which would be akin to a surgical strike to remove a cancerous tumor the size of a grapefruit.

As I felt the psychological weight that must have burdened Keith's shoulders at that time, I heard his voice from a distance. He continued this painful testimony from a Georgian operating plant's conference room from a decade ago as if we were living inside of a TV movie in that resounding baritone:

"So once we started up the conference call with the Delaware trio, I really got going. What I had suspected all along was turning out to be absolutely true. I began, with informing the phone crowd about my surprise trip to Georgia, because I was suspicious about how valid their overall Fiber Division's financials. I talked about my first hand knowledge of what our customers were saying about the dip in their own Earnings Per Share (EPS). We went through the painful confirmation of the taxi cab driver of the huge piles of fiber stored locally that just did not add up to the much smaller inventory numbers provided to me on their Division's balance sheet."

"So I told all of them I wanted to know who's plan it was? Was it these people down here in LaGrange, Georgia all on their own, that were sitting right in front of me? Or were they ordered to make these inaccurate entries by Corporate? If so, I want to know who gave them the order to do it? I pointed out that after our call, regardless of their answers, the internal auditor is going to put a team together and go through the financials of this plant in a forensic sort of way. So if none of them talked, he was SURE as sh*t going to figure this out! By that time I was pretty hot under the collar. I could see the blood draining from the plant manager and controller's faces sitting across from me at the conference table. One of them looked like they were going to lose their lunch as I went on."

"At that point, over the phone the General Manager (GM) of the entire division admitted that the two LaGrange plant employees were directed to do it by the Division Controller, because he himself had made them all do it. It was classic bullying from the top down."

I interjected, "So when I hear you say stuff like aberrant behavior usually has something to do with money, this would be a prime example! It makes weird numbers pop out that just don't make any sense."

With a nod of the head, Keith bravely carried on, "I asked the GM, why in the world would he do something like that? But Ahhh knew the answer to mah own question, it would be to earn their planned bonuses. To get themselves out of the mess the next year, they'd hafta figure out another fraud to offload all the sh*t ya couldn't sell cuz no one is buying! Since none of the product was recorded there wuz no trail, so it would be even easier to sell it on the sly, and personally pocket the cash!"

As the minister's daughter, I could hear the scripture verse reverberating between my ears, "For the <u>love</u> of money is the root of all evil, which while some coveted after...pierced themselves with many sorrows." So a key point is how do you work with money in your life without falling in love with it? Ahhh as the great Shakespeare bard wrote, "Therein lies the rub." Nations, institutions and most of all people have failed this test over and over.

Weirdly, who are the most famous, influential people in history? People who gave it all away, right? To name a few: Mother Theresa, Gandhi, Jesus Christ and his Disciples, the Buddha and Joan of Arc. Of course many wealthy people supported their visions turning them into realities. But we don't readily recall Joseph of Arimathea, the wealthy global tin oligarch, except for the fact that he provided the most infamous burial plot. Yet, we remember the name Jesus.

I started humming George Strait's applicable melody, mind you rather tunelessly, but nevertheless: "Just give it away."

*~ What we Cling to the Hardest
can Harm us the most ~*

THINGS ARE NOT OFTEN
AS THEY APPEAR

~ When it is all Flash, often there is no Cash ~

Keith's lonely soliloquy was painful:

"So I said, 'Well ok, I'm really disappointed that this happened. And there are going to be rather hard consequences as a result of this thang that's gonna happen here. This here plant manager is going to slow the run of this plant down to produce a product level that is needed to consistently reduce the inventory, but not to run it at a level that will result in a loss. I think we can get the outside auditors to agree to that, but we will have to see about it. I believe your numbers are huge in your overall fiber division, but hopefully it's small enough to NOT be a material weakness in the financials! We can't have an exception in the outside auditors' report cuz we will have a public outcry, and I certainly do want to try to avoid that kinda problem!' at least that's the gist of what I recall havin' to say," Keith ended resolutely.

As a CPA, I knew how bad this could have been. This kind of incident could be and actually was the death knell of many public companies. All it took was a few

Wall Street analysts ready to make an example out of one company, so that people didn't look elsewhere. For there are many variations on schemes that are perpetrated on the American public. Often the guilty love to point fingers at other offenders as a method to distract and deflect from a pocket full of money they themselves made on the sly.

As if reading my mind, Keith responded to my unspoken response, "It was these kinda things, that once I became CEO and it was my head alone on the chopping block, that I never slept well again. I didn't believe Tom, my predecessor, when he said those kinda things. But he was darn right. And ten years later, I still don't sleep right. You never get over it I guess." Keith muttered more to himself by this point.

At this point I was trying out for the first time a post-dinner coffee and liquor combination, which was weird. It kind of reminded me of rum cake, two things that didn't really go together. But in any event, the coffee got me perked up a bit so I could concentrate on the final death spiral of this fraud. After all the hard work by thousands of good people, and it could have all been lost in a puff a smoke from just a few people colluding and making poor choices to enrich themselves in the short run.

 The death of my first accounting firm felt like the sacrificial lamb to pay for the sins of the whole financial services world when they colluded with

Enron to perpetrate their accounting fraud on the American public. There were many implicit firms and actors across industry and government, so someone had to be put to death. Therefore the death of my first employer Arthur Andersen, Enron's external auditor, was still fresh in my rear view mirror. However, my personal antennae had always been triggered over Enron. Out of nowhere they were naming football stadiums, sponsoring super bowls and the like. It was too fast, there was some smoke and mirrors aspect to their story, you could sense it. No one could really explain what they did, it was similar to the sub-prime mortgage debacle that followed. The fraudsters played the age old "Emperor's New Clothes" trick. "You must be too stupid to understand these very sophisticated techniques." Enron was definitely a case to define my personal mantra: "All Flash, no cash."

My mind returned from its journey into the recent past to hear Keith wrapping up the final parts of his nightmare. He was in the Georgia conference room, wrapping up that phone call with the Division Manager and Controller up North in Wilmington, with the two local conspirators sitting across the wooden table from him. Keith surmised:

"I wrapped up that painful meeting with, 'I'm going to leave the plant now, and I will be back in Wilmington this afternoon. I expect that you two will wait for me to get back, so we can talk in person.

Don't go home until we have had our conversation.'
They agreed."

"The Plant manager and controller asked if they could
take me back to the airplane, which I agreed. On that
ride they told me how the plan had been hatched by
their bosses at their Fiber Division's headquarters
about three or four months previously. At that time
they all knew they were not going to Make Plan, and
no one was going to get a bonus. Initially the plant
guys had both objected, but they both were threatened
with their jobs by the two Division heads back at
Corporate, if they didn't do what they were told."

"Now to ensure that I had more than just hearsay to
go upon when I confronted the corporate heads when
I returned to Wilmington, they brought me a copy of
the "smoking gun" email demanding the plant guys'
specific performance. They wanted numbers that
matched their own false forecast of a real expansion in
diaper sales," Keith paused to collect his thoughts. I
could see the Scottish flush creeping up onto his face
as he began the final painful chapter.

"During the flight on the way home, I decided what
the consequences were going to be which began with
the immediate termination of the corporate based
Divisional General Manager and Controller who
demanded participation of their plant's suordinates in
the misstatements. Two, the internal forensic audit of
the plant occurred and that the accounting books and

records for the division were presented correctly. Three, when I prepared a video of my internal quarterly earnings statement to the employees, the following week, I would have a new segment. It would include the Georgia plant's manager and controller explaining what had happened, how they were wrong in following their direct reports' orders. But more importantly, it outlined the steps that employees should follow to elevate wrongdoing beyond their own management as whistleblowers."

I responded with, "This was a classic case of how collusion breaks down the planned separation of duties wasn't it? This is why the numbers people report separately to the CFO and not the Operations people. It also highlights the importance of a separate outlet for whistleblower employees. Since the operations guy was colluding with the numbers guy, they could effectively cook the books. But they had to bully their subordinates to get away with it! Even though it was painful, I think what you did was very valuable. In the long term, who knows how many other frauds you stopped by disclosing this one."

Nodding his head in agreement, Keith continued, "I promoted Janet Gray Sanders from another division to controller, effectively immediately. Besides being quite talented, she was as honest as the day is long. At the overall level, we were very fortunate that this fraud did not rise to the point of materiality. If I had ignored my instincts, for another few quarters, we may not have been so lucky. If it HAD resulted in a material weakness that was subsequently discovered by our external auditors it could have been death. Since we found it ourselves, came up with an enforceable solution, our auditors were pretty happy. They agreed with our terminations and promotions. Overall, it was a terrible experience, especially when I had to face the two Division leaders whose brainchild was the whole thang, then have security escort them from my office to their office to turn over all of their company items and work products before being escorted from the building."

Curiously I asked, "Well that was all the internal exposure, which is hard to imagine in and of itself. How did you communicate with the external world? Technically, they could have been arrested I'm sure. But I know that white collar crimes like this one are hard to get a jury to convict, as they are not easy to explain and are darn expensive to litigate…" my thoughts trailed off as I thought of varying scenarios.

"Yeah, you were right, pressing charges was a road we didn't want to travel. But we did have to prepare an announcement for the next day's local paper. We took the high road, naming the employees that had left to pursue other opportunities. Besides the external public, I also had to write a letter to the Board of Directors as an agenda item for our next meeting. I asked our General Internal Auditor to attend so he could answer any detailed questions they may have had regarding the whole awful affair."

~ Learn to Listen than act
on what your Tummy tells You ~

THE HOLY GRAIL

~ Ask questions,
who knows where it will Lead ~

The next time Keith and I got together was a few days later He was still in a hurricane evacuation mode. This session was a lot lighter after our last dinner with the cathartic painful regression into Keith's past. It seemed timely to share some exciting news that I had luckily received that day. One of the very connected, Atlanta law firms had supported my membership to The Buckhead Club. Now I didn't have time to wine and dine anyone, but Bernie, my direct report Boss (remember this was the matrix where I reported to about twenty-four bosses all over the country), reminded me how socialization was the Southern way here in Atlanta. This was important, especially for people like us Yankees, to fit in down here in the South, bless our hearts!

Sighing, I forked up the cash I didn't really have to join the club I didn't have time to attend and gave them my email address. Within a few short weeks, I got an email-newsletter from the club, which I probably only opened since I was just finding my way around my

new city. I generally don't even sign up for
newsletters, as I never have time to read them. But for
some reason that day I did.

It was an offer to purchase four tickets to the world
famous Masters' Annual Golf Tournament for the
entire week! For you non-golfers out there, this
mecca-event was held annually in Augusta, Georgia
about ninety miles East of Atlanta, on the border of
Georgia and South Carolina at the "home of golf"
where Bobby Jones turned it into hallowed ground.

The offer included, the use of a local home at the
famous course's gates as a social gathering place.
Augusta's local residents had figured out a quite
successful entrepreneurial solution regarding the world
descending on their small town once a year. They
rented out their homes to the press and golfing
maniacal public for the week. The short term rental
program was sizzling so much, that many homeowners
paid their entire year's mortgages and real estate taxes
with the one week's pull of rental proceeds. Now this
was way before AirBnB.com was ever conceived. So
people were accomplishing this with a lot more spit
and shoe leather, so it was pretty impressive.

At the time, I was not a golfer. One day I aspired to
be, when my mortgage, children's private school
tuition, nanny and retirement had all been paid for. So
this was not yet that time! Yet I was an avid sports fan,
and I knew I would enjoy the spectacle of the Masters'

up close. This was when Phil Mickelson and Tiger
Woods were sparring for golf's major trophies.

I ran around the corner to Bernie's office. I asked him
if he thought this was a joke. I knew how all the
Atlanta people talked about this tournament as the
ultimate on their personal bucket lists. In the short
time of my residency, I had heard multiple tales from
the locals of how no matter what, they could never
get tickets. It had become a fruitless chase. All that
being said, I didn't really believe this was a real email.
It had to be a scam.

Bernie said, "Email them right now and get your name
in line! They are probably already gone! You can take
a bunch of clients and expense them through the firm,
and I will approve it! This is like the Holy Grail
around here, Erica!" That's why I didn't really believe
it, I told Bernie. Now these tickets were as much as
my month's home expenses, so I was certainly not
contemplating purchasing these whatsoever if it wasn't
for the good of the firm and I was reimbursed. With
Bernie's blessing, I hit send. So, that is how I obtained
four tickets per day for the entire Masters' Golf
Tournament all expenses paid. It was the year of
Tiger Woods' famous hole-out chip-in on Amen
Corner.

~ If you don't Ask, you will never Know ~

DON'T MAKE ASSUMPTIONS

~ As humans, we can't always see another's Heart, but we can certainly Share our Own ~

So I knew Keith was a big time golfer, I thought it would be a perfect thing to ask him to attend at least one of the days with me. After all he had been a guest of my firm many a big-time client of the firm. Keith had treated me to so many remarkable wine and dining experiences, it would be fun to be able to reciprocate in a unique way. What else can you give a Renaissance man that has the world by the tail, besides a new experience?

Then I planned to give the rest of the tickets to my contact, Doug, at Delta Air Lines. That way Doug could distribute the tickets as he saw fit among the team of executives that we provided financial planning services. After all, I didn't want to tiptoe through the minefield of their corporate politics, Doug was a lot closer to the ground, he would know better how to best manage the internal rivalries.

Even though it was the Fall, and the Masters was a long ways away the following spring, I thought it was a good time to lighten up the conversation with fun social planning after the intense fraud narrative. Little did I know the can of worms I would open, when I thought I would be giving a great gift. When I asked if Keith had ever been to Augusta before, boy was I in for a surprise.

Keith lit up like a Christmas Tree. "Erica, I tell you what, Augusta is the most special place in the world for golfers. I've had the good fortune of playing the course over a dozen times."

In complete surprise, I responded, "Are you kidding me? I was hoping there was at least one thing in the world that you hadn't done yet, that I could organize for you! Of all the golfers I've met in my life, none of them have been to Augusta. And here you are, not only have you been there, you've played there multiple times!"

With a smile, Keith replied, "Come now, Erica. There are plenty of things I haven't done yet. And I am glad, because I look forward to doing them with you."

Now that just made my heart melt. I couldn't really hear what else Keith was saying for a few moments as the blood rushed through my ears.

He continued, "But let me tell you why this was true. When I was working at Hercules, we were fortunate enough to have a really unique relationship with some very well known members of that golf club that went back some fifty years, Ahhh believe. Long before mah time there. Now there wuz a man named Charlie Yates, who was a very close friend of Bobby Jones. En Charlie Yates-ez' sis-tuh married a man that became CEO of Hercules. So, that created an opportunity for Hercules to take customers and on an annual golf outing at Augusta National! Ahh remember every hole I played there, every time."

"The very first time, Ahh recall Tom came to my office and asked me something like whatta are you doing the next two days. When I reminded him, I had a lot going on, Tom said something like well, ok but I thought you might be interested in rearranging so you could accompany me to Augusta for a couple days of golf! Can you believe that? At that point, I told him I will change my whole calendar! Let me tell you it was surreal standing on the first tee, with Charlie Yates. At Augusta, every foursome of guests is required to have at least one member, and we were honored to play with Charlie. What a gentleman he wuz."

"We were so fortunate to be able to have two or three foursomes every year. Normally it would be a week or two after the Masters' Tournament so the greens would be rolled so fast! Like lighting! We began each event, arriving for lunch at the club house, playing golf in the afternoon, cocktails in the cabins where we were staying, then dinner at the clubhouse. The next morning, we would have breakfast in the cabin where we were staying, followed by golf in the morning, lunch, immediately followed by our departure. Every year I was there we stayed in the famous Butler cabin, because that is where they give out the green jacket to the winner of the Masters Tournament in front of the fireplace. Normally, that same room is where breakfast was served every morning. One of my favorite memories of these trips, was the Negro spiritual singing group, they were amazing."

Now I realized we were in the pea patch of some of Keith's happiest memories in life. He whispered sotto voce, "You can just imagine what it was to play through Amen corner the first time. I was really proud of myself as I was able to average par on those three holes. I bogeyed eleven, parred twelve, and birdied thirteen!"

It was then that I began to realize that the only unique gifts I could give Keith was something I invented on my own. Creativity would become my necessary mother of invention. At the end of the day, I gave all the tickets away to my Atlantean Delta employee clientele, whom never had the chance to walk golf's local sacred grounds. Instead, when the Masters Tournament rolled around, I jumped on a Delta flight down to Palm Beach to visit my favorite client and own dear Braveheart.

~ Practice sharing your Treasure,
so you Find your own Soulful Path ~

PHONE CALLS & WHITE TIES

~ *Turn Off the Technology*
and let Humanity fade Away ~

After a few months of this sassy phone and plane relationship, we had successfully built a secret life together. While the world whirled around us, we went within ourselves and discovered a deep, mystical world. We knew it was there, but it had never been fully accessible without the other. When there are no witnesses, and there are just two of you in the room, looking into each other's eyes, nose to nose, the sounds of humanity fade away and there is no one else. If you allow it, there becomes this truth between you that is a sacred bond of trust. Others don't realize it exists, until they try to interfere, then it is that one secret smile, nod or wink. Then this invisible force field arises around the two of you and no intruder can pass. There is this bond and its name is called love.

I had saved a voicemail on my Blackberry- and I would replay it over and over of Keith's voice. He left it for me late one night when I slept. A gift the next morning:

"I have lived an amazing life that I can't even believe sometimes, but all of it means nothing if I am alone. All of my accomplishments, they are meaningless if I can't enjoy the fruits of my labor with someone. And I want to share it with you. The only thing that could be better is to have you with me to enjoy each day, as the crown jewel of my life…"

With that final phrase, I cried each time during this private reverie. To be valued like this, to be loved like this, for myself alone, by such a man, I wept.

~ Each one of us hold Deep, endless Pools of Mystery awaiting Discovery ~

MEETING THE FAMILIES

~ When you have Found each others' Secret
shores, there is Nothing left to Fear ~

We were tiptoeing around our families not ready to disrupt the status quo until we were both confident in the fact that "we were it".

We began slowly with introductions closest to home with Hannah and Chloe. After all they would be the ones living with Keith. I read many books on divorce by this point. But I think the most pragmatic manual on the long standing impact on the children is Judith Wallerstien's seminal work, *The Unexpected Legacy of Divorce: A Twenty-Five Year Landmark Study.* Her work brought awareness, sometimes quite uncomfortable, to the immediate and long lasting effect of divorce on children. She also documented how transparency and honest recognition of all of the pragmatic changes for the kids needed to be recognized as big deals, because they were. Stability is key, but how do you affect that? The age and gender of each child also impacts their response to the divorce.

In my words, you must learn to practice empathy for your children and see the effects on them through their eyes, or you will undermine their trust in you. You already are impacting their world view, but without empathy it will be in an even more profoundly negative way, especially in their own future adult relationships.

So we started with small steps. One Friday night, Keith checked into the hotel and met up with Rufus the driver. As they made their journey to my home in Mableton, a small suburb due West from midtown Atlanta, I began to get ready for a date with Keith. Four year old Chloe sat on the wide bathroom counter next to me and began applying make-up to her own cherub cheeks. She decided she needed to put on an outfit too. When she returned from her closet, she had selected her two piece cheerleading outfit that she had worn for Halloween. Then we did her hair in two pony tails. I realized she wanted to go on the date too, so we talked about how this was a grown up dinner but she would meet Keith when he arrived at the house to pick me up.

Hannah bounced through the bathroom. She was apparently born with invisible springs embedded in her feet. She pirouetted in continuous circles on her bare toes. In my mind's eye, I still see her wearing her favorite cotton-knit red skort and matching shirt, as she chattered about her upcoming sleepover at Jackie's house across the cul-de-sac.

One of the small things I noticed about each child, especially after the divorce, was that they both gravitated towards a few comfy outfits when at home and stuck with them. Even if they wanted to wear it every day, we just washed them more often. I viewed it as something in their purview that they could control. If they couldn't control bigger options that their parents made, they could be in charge of this.

For awhile, Hannah perpetually wore this red one outfit. She had always gravitated to red wardrobe choices; now she was powering down on the color even more so. Hannah's preferred color choice triggered some of my first initial investigatory forays into alternative forms of self-healing. What did the color red mean? Why was it so appealing to her? I found a few books about the color spectrum and how the colors of the rainbow were associated with the seven human energy chakras. Today in 2019, the term chakra has seeped further into the American lexicon. But in the early 2000's, I hadn't started my daily yoga regimen yet, so I had no clue.

I was surprised to find that the acronym for the colors of the rainbow that we memorized as children, ROY G BIV applied to the human body too. The most ancient written records regarding chakras are first discussed in the ancient Indian texts called The Vedas, written before Christ. Red is assigned to the base or root chakra, located at the base of our spines. It is considered an earthy grounding color that helps return and root us in reality. Hmmm.

According to this ancient tradition the human body has seven energy centers or chakras that occur from the base of our spine to the top of our skull. There is a color associated with each center too which match the order of the color spectrum that we sometimes see naturally occurring in rainbows: red, orange, yellow, green, blue, indigo and violet. So I meditated on the story of Noah and the rainbow, and I came to believe that there was another deeper meaning to this world flood narrative.

On the other hand, Chloe preferred a dark pink skort with a sky blue shirt with little ice cream cones appliqued across her chest. Ironically, I realized the shirt was one of the souvenir items, I purchased that fateful trip to Palm Beach when I first looked into Keith's kind eyes. Over the months of the intricate dance of family integration, I would look at these little ice cream cones as a symbol of hope that we were somehow going to complete this transition process successfully.

When I asked Hannah that first night, if she wanted to delay her departure and meet Keith beforehand, she was quite nonchalant and didn't want to miss out on one minute with her gaggle of new Atlanta friends. So we left it like that, why turn this first introduction into a negative?

When Keith pulled up in Rufus' black town car, I had Chloe on my right hip. From under her heavy dark bangs, she looked solemnly into Keith's eyes as if she could see our combined futures. Suddenly shy, she rested her head on my shoulder peering out from underneath one eyelid before giving us both a peck on the cheek and waving good-bye.

Approaching this new family combination, I had worked feverishly with my counselor, Larry Adams. Not only was he a master academically in his field, but he had the empathy gene. He recommended a child counselor Dr. King to work with my daughters. Chloe was quite put off by Dr. King, "Mommy that's a weird name!"

"Whaddya mean Clo? Dr. King is fairly simple.."

"Mommy! Dr. King is a woman, her name should be Dr. Queen! Don't you know anything?"

Trying to keep my laugh to myself, I was relieved to know it wasn't the issue of talking to a therapist, it was her erroneous name that was throwing a wrench into Chloe's mind works. And how do you answer that question?

Each day when I left work, I would often talk to Keith on my half hour drive home- he would be standing in his swimming pool, with the newspaper and business reports spread around him, and he would talk me home. We would give each other reports about what we had accomplished that day, until I arrived pulled into the driveway.

We had reached a solid decision that when we were ready to choose to start a life with each other, we were just going to choose, without asking anyone else's permission. This was somewhat counter to what the "experts" said on talk shows and in books, but it rang true to us. We talked about it a lot with Dr. Larry, who encouraged us to find our own way. He was quite emphatic about this. "If you attempt to obtain your children's permissions and approvals, don't be surprised if you are disappointed. This is true whether they are Keith's adult children or Erica your juvenile children. They will view your choice to marry as an inconvenience if not an outright interference in their own relationships with each of you. The moral high ground is for you to choose for yourselves. There is obvious risk if you offload the burden of choice onto others. One could argue that it might not even be intellectually honest."

And with that I felt quite free. It was no longer a performance to gain others' approvals. I had lived my whole life for others' expectations of me, that it was exhilarating to suddenly find I knew exactly what I wanted to do, and I was the only person that I needed to seek permission! Wow!

At the same time, Keith began to weigh changing his life. At first, we thought it would be easier for adult children to adjust, for they weren't living with us. But that is not necessarily reality. If anything, the adult sophistication comes with a lot more wariness and skepticism. And they also came with wives and children, complicated.

I think the fact that we both had physically moved made us both a bit more free-wheeling in our decision making. Keith had moved from city to city throughout his entire career. He called himself a fix up clean up sorta guy. Of course, he was downgrading the fact that he was speaking at the executive C-Suite level, but it still held true. He would get hired to come in and clean up messy financial situations, so he had worked the merry go round counter clock-wise from Delaware, Pittsburgh, Niagara Falls, Connecticut, Rumson, New Jersey and then ended up where he started in Wilmington, Delaware. Therefore, upon retirement, it felt fairly natural for him to go find another place to live.

 I know if I had still been living in my Greater Philadelphia life where everyone had known me for a very long time, it would have been hell. But here in Atlanta, where I had started my single Mom life, the only people who knew of me were acquaintances at work. So my geography definitely shaped my history and made my decision making even simpler.

Yet, I did continue to receive emails, phone calls and actual written letters from friends, co-workers, exneighbors and yes even one minister telling me I was woefully wrong to execute my divorce, but at least it was from afar. They had to get on a plane to try to drag me back, so I felt fairly safe. Even so, at least one threatened to kidnap my daughters and take them back up North "where they rightfully belonged with their father in his original habitat", so I didn't feel extraordinarily safe. More like Bette Midler "from a distance" safe. So, it just felt best to keep my head down and go about my own business.

There was this point in time, where Keith and I were goofing off, rolling around, falling off the couch in front of the fireplace in my new home in Atlanta, when we ended up nose to nose on the floor and Keith looked dead in my eyes and said "I if I could, I would have given it all up for you."

Brings tears to my eyes now.

One of the big hurdles that Keith and I had to overcome was time, in its many splendored variations. First we didn't have a lot of it to spend with each other based on all of our competing obligations. I felt we had to make the most of every minute. Two, we were coming from different generations and different worlds, so we were starting from ground zero in each others' lives. So on one of our many check in phone calls, I had a surprise request.

"Keith, please bring any yearbooks, photo albums, whatever you wanted to share about your personal life."

"What? Really?"

I didn't know it at the time, but Keith's passions and interests had been ignored for a very long time. In fact, his personal historical roots in South Carolina, were stomped on quite frequently, so my request was all the more surprising. In a last ditch effort to save his unhappy first marriage, came when he retired from business. He was still relatively young in business years, and therefore was offered a final feather in his cap as the Dean of South Carolina's Business School, after completing an arduous interview process. This was the very school where he had already been named as an outstanding Alum, where he placed first in his MBA class.

Sadly, his first wife, went AWOL over the very thought of moving to South Carolina. So he painstakingly rejected the magical opportunity to finish his career by reinvesting in the very place that launched him in his business endeavors.

So one afternoon, we sat for hours pouring over his college yearbooks. It felt very cathartic, but I didn't know how very deeply healing it was for Keith until further down the road. His personal heritage and history had been suppressed for a very long time.

Suddenly, here I was, and I wanted to hear his story, really a tale beyond description. He was one out of hundreds in his high school class that went to the Northeast and broke through. Keith's story was of a David and Goliath type ilk. He had worked with legions of hallowed names, both companies and individuals, from around the world. But somehow, someway he had magically stayed true to himself. That fact was truly breathtaking to me. He had somehow saved his own soul, but he was still tearfully alone. Maybe that was why? He wouldn't sell out? The Empath in me wanted to understand him. I was all ears. Thus began another level of our storytelling. It was documented by photographs and family trees scribbled haphazardly on napkins.

The idea of connecting through archives of personal documents at each of our tête-à-têtes was so fun. It worked to provide us with a sense of time and place. It was when we were reviewing his yearbooks, that I began to realize what a force of nature Keith was from a very early age. He was President of this, and top pledge of that and Outstanding Senior and Officer of his fraternity, the list went on and on.

I didn't understand it at first, but as the Carolinian stories unfolded, Keith was like a flower opening to the sun for the first time in years. How was this possible? I had spent hours listening to Keith regale me with amazing stories in his adult business career, where he had literally set the whole world on fire, then

doused out other flammable frauds before they
burned down the village, created new supplies of
industrial raw metals, all without him flinching a facial
muscle.

How was this true? This is when I came to find, what
is sadly most often the case. Keith's original core had
been suppressed and often downright denigrated. He
spent his professional life living and working amongst
strangers in the Greater Northeast, many of whom
reminded him on a daily basis of how "demonstrably
debased" he was for being born in the Lesser South.
Sadly, some of those whom he was closest to, derided
him the most. It wasn't until the close of his career,
that he found someone in me that was willing to listen
to these unbelievable war stories. How can one climb
to the top of Mt. Everest and then be told you didn't
deserve it because you weren't born in the right
geography? Was this really America?

As we continued to unravel the strange fictions that
we were force fed, Keith made a surprise social
introduction of me at the University of South
Carolina. Initially, we went to attend a University
event. I must have driven over from Atlanta and
Keith came in from Florida, and we met in Cahl-Lum-
Bee-Ahh, South Carrow-Line-Ahh, otherwise known
as Columbia, South Carolina.

On the spur of the moment, Keith called Dr. John
and Norma Palms, the current President and First

Lady of the University of South Carolina! Suddenly, we were invited to their home for cocktails and hors d'oeuvres.

I never met anyone like Norma; she was a force of nature with whom you just fell in love. She made things happen without batting an eyelash, even with an injured foot elevated above her head on a boatload of cushions, while she sailed right through the social sea of asking all about you, how you were doing, and what did your Mother think of all this. They were an unbelievable partnership of husband and wife. Not only was John the President of the University but he was also a nuclear physicist. And Norma could return a battleship blindfolded to her port of call, to the town of her birth, Charleston, South Carolina.

So one blustery winter day, while I was driving around on the streets of Atlanta, valiantly fighting traffic and clocks to find a client's home office, Keith called to ask if I would accompany him to the Caroliniana Ball. Now this was an annual event. It was quite formal and this year it was being held at The Grove Park Inn in Asheville, North Carolina, a few hours Northeast of my home in Atlanta.

Hamlin, Keith's best friend, whom I met that very first fateful night at the Palm Beach Grill, asked Keith if we would like to attend this Southern Cotillion of Manners replete with resplendent white tie. Now not being raised in the South nor in a setting of any formal sense, this nuance of social splendor was already lost on me. To me, white tie meant the guy wore a tux, and he chose to wear a white tie instead of a black one. Wow, he had an option in the stringent limited options of the required tuxedo uniform!

Wrong! White tie, meant wearing the whole giddyup! "Tails" on the tuxedo jacket, white gloves, an actual white tie, a vest. And shockingly in the South, Keith told me some of his friends owned their own "white tie whole thang" and some even wore a top hat and fitted it out with a cane! What?

I didn't really believe him, until he started complaining about how he had a coupla tuxedos, but no white tie, he for damn sure wasn't going to buy one for this damn event. Which of course I asked the obvious question of why were we going?

That's when we got into the history of the whole place, The Grove Park Inn. We took our time driving there, Keith drove up from South Florida to Atlanta to pick me up that Friday afternoon. From Atlanta, our plan was to complete the road trip to Asheville, North Carolina, which was a few hours away.

On that weekend, he started a loving tradition of picking things out for me to wear as a gift. That day, when I climbed into his Mercedes, he had this sleek black sunglasses case that he handed to me to open.

Now I have to tell you, I didn't accessorize at that time whatsoever. I didn't own one pair of sunglasses, because whatever budget I had for clothes, the money was going to go into one important signature piece that could be integrated into my existing color palette and wardrobe. When I opened the leather crafted box there was this beautiful pair of subtly tinted rose-colored sunglasses by Salvatore Ferragamo that I still have to this day. I was actually afraid to touch them, they were so beautiful. What had I done? This was not a world I easily fit into. What if I wrecked it?

With that very thoughtful gesture, we began our winding drive through the South. We took a minor detour to drive through Abbeville, the small town where Keith was born and grew up. We saw road signs for other oddly named towns such as Due West and Ninety-Six, that triggered flashbacks to my youth. My Pop's high school basketball team came down for a summer road trip to get ready for states, and played in all these uniquely named places. A stark contrast to the urban jungle of Chester, Pennsylvania. I heard my Dad's ebullient voice echoing in my ears, "Err (my family's abbreviated nickname for me), It's God's Country down there." And it truly was.

As we wandered North over the border into the wagging tail tip of Western North Carolina, the grade of the road increased as we started our ascent into the Smoky Mountains. And they do have this purplish haze in the distance. The flora of these mountains are some of the most complex in breadth of plant forms. Some scientists are beginning to think that due to this the Appalachian mountain range is in fact the oldest range in the world, verifying local Native American myths.

This long winding ascent definitely gave me the feeling of slowly climbing a stairway to heaven. It was up into the cumulus clouds. Lines from a poem I had worked over the years ambled through my mind:

> *The sun reflects back and laughs at our song ...the clouds*
> *scudding by whisper you're free.*

Yes, I felt like I was breaking out of some of the boxes that I had built for myself over the years. I found that I had had the choice all along to free myself to find the real me. It just took me awhile to realize it.

~ Don't be afraid of Breaking some of the Boxes
Holding you In ~

AMAZING TECHNICOLOR ASHEVILLE

~ Have fun in your Labeling,
make it Memorable ~

As we approached Asheville, the beltway surrounding it was a miniature of the Atlanta circle. But apparently, the entrance ramps were influenced by Evel Knievel as they were built dangerously short. Each one was more like a launching pad, that the locals used to slingshot their cars into the parade of oncoming traffic. It was a rude awakening after our romantic road trip. Suddenly, jammed together exit signs were flying by every quarter mile. Locals weaved among the annoying tourists' cars not familiar yet with the jarring shifting lane patterns. Besides the NC license plates and the aggressive driving patterns, you could spot the locals' cars, because of the numerous homegrown bumper stickers they applied. "Keep Asheville Weird." "Welcome to Asheville. Now Go Home." "She-Ville." And some others that can't be repeated here.

Even from the highway, the views of Asheville are beautiful as it is built into a shallow valley tucked into the Blue Ridge Mountains. The rolling hills were decorated with a plethora of multi-colored trees that one could call Mother Nature's version of Joseph's Amazing Technicolor Dreamcoat. I only half-believed the picture postcards of the ephemeral purple haze clothing the Smoky Mountains, until I saw it that day for myself. It was quite mystical.

We somehow exited from the busy freeway safely and we were suddenly in a shaded world of tree lined streets where Colonial and Tudor Revival homes dotted the landscape interspersed with a smattering of bungalows. The streets continued to narrow as we wound our way up towards the resort. My pragmatic self wondered how many man hours went into the presumably gargantuan task of raking up all of the leaves each Autumn.

As we rounded the last curve in the road we were greeted by the Grove Park Inn's guardsman regaled in a period uniform from another chapter in time. The spacious cobbled courtyard is breathtaking it itself. As one enters, the sheer scale of the Inn is imposing even though it was built in 1913. One's eye is drawn to the uncut massive granite boulders that were used in the facade as opposed to a more traditional smooth bricks and mortar. Each unique boulder juts out in its own natural direction. The dormered red tiled roof rippled free form. The solidness of the building with the capture of movement through the uncut stone and undulating roof reminded one of Mother Nature herself. The conundrum of solidity and constant movement, like the ocean itself.

As we entered the resort's lobby, I caught my breath in wonder. The room is massive in scale, height and width. On the far sides are matching fireplaces of massive scale, where a person could easily walk into each one. Their facades were also built with the uncut local granite boulders, giving one the feeling that one rock could suddenly tumble out onto the floor. One could imagine, that us humans had mistakenly entered a giant's home where he was entertaining himself with a game of Pick-up Sticks, but instead of wood, he was using large boulders.

But the lobby is also a look through room. The whole back wall opens onto a descending terrace. It serves as a window on the world framing the Blue Ridge Mountains view, with their iconic purple haze. I was transfixed, I didn't really believe the Smokies really were that smoky.

After sending our bags to the room, we sat down at a table on the Sunset Terrace, for some appetizers and a cocktail before our late dinner. The view of the setting sun over the Smokies was just incredible. I loved this place already. Seeing Keith in the context of his Carolina roots, brought deeper layers of him to the forefront. It explained so much, the subtle manners and gestures, the many Southern colloquialisms that didn't make logical sense but provided hilarious color commentary to illustrate points. "It's raining harder than pouring piss out of a boot on a flat rock." Why would anyone ever pee into a boot, I am not sure, but the visual doesn't leave much to the imagination. I think the Southern Charm became a distinctive power tool in Keith's career toolbelt. He could present a soft side that offset his tough as nails reputation. The contrast was utterly disarming.

~ When one Returns Home,
Reflection comes Naturally ~

SWITCHING GEARS

~ It can be Painful in Practice
to Rise Above it All ~

As we sat enjoying each other's company, I could feel the glares coming from the table next to us, where two busy body women were staring me down. I could hear the one woman say (as I am sure she planned) to the other, "I just don't get it! I just don't get the whole older man thing! I mean really who does THAT?"

It was a jolt bringing me back to the present. Really? Would she be happier if I was sitting here with her theoretical twenty-two year old son? Let's just call a spade a shovel, she was miserable and I was not. Apparently, I had stolen a horse from her fields of opportunity. Misery does love company, and will attempt to create a larger field of anguish all around it.

It is amazing to me how opinionated people can be, about others living outside of their personally crafted molds. Who actually feels happy living inside another's expectant mold anyway? I would expect one just starts to grow moldy.

If someone is trying to force you back into their carefully derived lanes, beware! Learn from the notes of my journey here, your bliss will roll off of you in supersonic waves. Your friends and others will not necessarily be happy for you. You might have to downshift into a lower gear on your All-Terrain Vehicle, make a hard right turn into the nearby fields where you can carve a new trail into the sunset. And heed the biblical warning, whatever you do, don't look back!

Therefore, throughout my life I've attempted to outright ignore the presence of such rude people, as I don't really believe in wasting my energy on a pointless argument. I like to pretend that I am above these nosy judgments, no matter how much they hurt. I also know that once I started down the road of retorts, I can quickly switch into another gear of anger that is not easy for me to control and continues to smolder like hot coals for a long time before extinguishing itself, which is never good.

But Keith on the other hand is a bird of another feather, he can flash to anger when needed and settle right back down to normal. With a start, I realized Keith too had picked up on this foray into our personal yard. He looked right into the chirper's eyes and barked,

"Whudd YOU looken at?"

Her friend, covered her own gaping mouth in shock. The chatty-cathy, who couldn't keep her opinions to herself, flushed beet red with embarrassment at being called out, and began to say something like, "Well, I've never been spoken to…"

When Keith interrupted her at another notch up the decibel scale:

"My Momma didn't raise no fool! And she also raised me to never be rude…. FIRST!"

As Keith's speaking voice can carry across the street, one more notch on his decibel scale registers on the same level as that old back porch dinner gong that rings throughout the neighborhood. Sudden silence spread across the terrace as other tables turned and stared. All of a sudden our opinionated neighbor was so uncomfortable, she grabbed her purse and ran for the restroom.

All my years of self-imposing my mantra of "don't make a scene," vanished as I observed Keith go right to the root cause of the conflict. Oh to be so immediate and honest, maybe one day. As is often the case when I witness conflict, I nervously let out a giggle. Then I couldn't stop laughing. We were beginning to already unconsciously read each other's thoughts. Keith answered my unspoken question, "You may remember how I told you the Mahlerism, 'Swat Annoying Flies Early?' That was one of the techniques that Walt Mahler taught me at his manager sessions. If you want to stop a behavior from ever happening again, the very first time someone behaves badly, call them out on it immediately. Make them so uncomfortable that they never do it to you again."

All I could muster was, "Wow, it certainly worked!" I hoped that one day I have the nerve to do it if necessary. I thought of all my circular pointless conversations with various people over the years talking around "The Thing" instead of just coming out with it.

My Braveheart not only defended us, he taught me an important life lesson that I still struggle with to this day. Suddenly, others judgments were quickly receding into the rearview mirror. It was very freeing to me. Often as women, we tend to over burden our friends with unwanted opinions and advice. I felt born again. As we were now preparing to walk the social gauntlet at this formal event, debuting as a couple with some of Keith's friends, this throw down was just what I needed to get my courage ginned up.

Conspiratorially, I leaned across the table and with a big grin and mischievously said, "Let's go raise some more hell."

Laughing Keith agreed, "Screw em if they can't take a joke."

~ Directness is often the Best Offense ~

ASSUMPTIONS

~ Physical proximity can be the most Disarming Opening in a Conversation ~

Over a number of months, we spent hours in truth telling, nose to nose, eye to eye. When apart, we'd chatter on traffic jam phone calls as I drove my Atlanta client circuit. Or after the girls' bedtime story hour, we would fall asleep on midnight phone calls.

Pretty soon, we had turned over every rock in each other's garden, opened every closet door to view the skeletons. Once we let in the daylight of empathetic understanding, things didn't seem so overwhelming. We felt safe. There was now no story left to be told by unhappy others that would be capable of driving a wedge between us. After forging this important emotional bond, we now trusted each other implicitly. We began to look around with new eyes wide open.

We talked logistics: living with my two young daughters, Keith's two adult sons with young families of their own, the X factor of living six hundred miles apart in two different states. We talked about all the What-Ifs, health risks, my career, Keith's remaining business responsibilities, our personal faiths, everything.

By the end of these conversations, we came up with a second golden rule, we planned to live by. Make good assumptions, until proven otherwise. And with that every decision felt pretty easy. When we believed and acted with each other's best interests at heart, we honored each other. We were very gentle and careful, talking slowly and rationally on how we thought a decision may affect the other. And in that we respected each other in our decision making processes, which continued to build yet a greater trust. Living life with each other was fast becoming an implicit presumption. In fact, life without each other was even harder to contemplate.

~ Make Good Assumptions,
until Proven Otherwise ~

THE DEEP END

~ One has to dive in Deep
to uncover Buried Treasure ~

After dinner that first evening at the Grove Park, we eventually found our way into their highly acclaimed, newly built spa. It was quite cunningly designed to fit into the rolling terrain. The hotel was initially built with the hill descending behind the original structure. Recently the builders retrofitted the spa into the sturdy granite bedrock sprawling down the hill. You actually went down an elevator into the earth to enter the spa. If you have ever been in a cave or down in a mine, there is a change to the pressure in your ears. You feel securely safe. If one pays attention, you quickly realize there is no vibration that we learn to ignore in high rises or quickly framed houses, But yet once you were down inside the mountain and entered the spa, if you kept walking through to the pool, one suddenly came face to face with that Royal Purple View again. It was like a walk out basement, down but out. The massive infinity type pool opened onto that horizon with the carpet of trees creeping into the distance looking for the edge.

We came together in the deep end of the pool like two whispering children, giggling that no one knew our secrets. And yes it was quite metaphorical because we knew we were in deep. Neither one of us wanted to go back to the way things were before. It was time for the next chapter.

So with that, we paddled over to the edge of the pool and looked out into the darkened sky. From this location, we could see Nature's original muse as she must have posed for Van Gogh when he captured her beauty in his masterpiece: *Starry Night*. So many of the stars and constellations, it was as if we were looking up into our own personal observatory, like the interior of a teapot dome.

Keith looked into my eyes and said, "Are you ready?"

And with a flourish, Keith reached into his swim trunks' pocket and pulled out the engagement ring he had chosen for me! At first that was terrifying, as I imagined it floating out of his pocket and down the pool drain! But then I flushed with relief, that we hadn't lost it in the pool, which would have had to be a bad omen right? It was then, I could finally relax and enjoy this beautiful moment with my Braveheart.

How did we get here?

Somehow it had all started with taxes and business then we ended up under the stars in the Blue Ridge Mountains planning our life merger. Clearly we were rocking the system before we even got started, when random strangers felt a need to comment on our togetherness. Now others' judgments seemed superfluous, we were making decisions based on our two opinions, and that was all that mattered.

As Keith held me in his strong embrace, we admired the beautiful, oval cut diamond together. It had an old world setting, that Keith had designed with the jeweler that included two trillions on the sides of the oval. It was truly one of a kind, and it felt like it represented us, because we sure didn't fit any known format either! And we privately really liked that.

Discreetly, I bent my left thumb tip inward to touch the back of the engagement ring's band encircling my ring finger. I wanted to ensure that I still had my magic charm that would help light my way through our first weekend, surrounded by Keith's friends immersed in Southern ways.

~ Implicit Mutual Trust
will Carry you a Long way ~

NORTHERN AGGRESSION

~ *Embrace Yourself* ~

As we entered the cavernous hall, somewhere in the subterranean levels of the resort, my stomach flipped over in a flurry of nervous energy. I normally didn't get butterflies, because I think I carry all my anxiety in my throat and mouth area. Normally, my teeth are clenched together, with my jaw locked, and my neck is involuntarily contracted. Obviously not a comfortable way to be; I'm still trying to unlearn these well worn habits. So maybe my nervous energy doesn't escape my clenched jaws too often to make a downward gastric trek.

On the fly last week, I had stormed through a mall on the way to a client meeting, and found an evening gown. It was made from soft crushed velvet in a deep garnet hue. The straps looked unique in that they were metal worked into a filigree pattern, but they also dug into my shoulders after awhile, so that was definitely uncomfortable. But I loved how the velvety folds draped over my chest and hips. In my view, it was much more flattering than some other shapes I'd worn. As part of the white tie expectations, Keith had warned me that many of the ladies would be wearing white elbow length gloves.

What? Gloves? Where do you even buy a pair? And this was way back before when Amazon was still only an online BOOK store sensation. They weren't the global world's online Turkish Bazaar yet. Thankfully, with some hints from Keith I was able to find some at a Tuxedo Rental shop for sale. What the heck?

So that night, we strolled down to our coming out party, with a bunch of random strangers, and even more strangely I was wearing elbow length gloves for the only time in my long-legged life.

We had come at the invitation of Hamlin, Keith's dearest friend from Palm Beach, who was there with his wife. Hamlin was originally from Greenville, South Carolina, and basically knew all five hundred guests from some point in his wide ranging social life. He was one of those genuine Irishmen that had a sixth sense about people, not only did everyone know him, but everyone loved him. And Hamlin, God Bless His Soul, was one of the few people that just KNEW when he saw us together. And as it happened, if you read my first book in this series already, Hamlin was there that very first night that I met Keith in the flesh. So it was only apropo that he was there to provide his Irish Blessing on our official engagement.

Being raised as I was in the randomness of my upbringing, I had no idea that so many people could know so many people in one place at one time. I was used to isolationist urbanity, where no one makes eye contact and everyone pretends they are walking around in a bubble while simultaneously rubbing elbows with multiple people.

Quite suddenly, Keith was eye to eye, with a tall man with a full head of silver gray hair. Quickly it became apparent that Bill was one of Keith's closest childhood friends! They were laughing, slapping each other on their tuxedo-ed backs. After Keith and Bill graduated high school, they had gone their separate ways for college. Once Keith began his business career in the Greater Northeast, their orbits spun even further apart.

 Bill was trying to catch up on decades and was now trying to figure out what had happened to Keith's first wife. It was suddenly crystal clear, she had never hit it off with Keith's childhood friends.

"Whatever is go-yin awn? Now Keith, how is it possible this lovely lady is spending time with you? I-ahh need to enlighten her about the real you, and warn her off before it is too late!" Bill was joking and laughing with clear happiness to have his dear friend by his side again.

And as the men exchanged loving insults, I was suddenly surrounded by Southern women who were raised in charm schools that I could only imagine from reading in novels, and I was terrified. Suddenly, I decided there is no way I can fake my way through this, so I am going back to my roots or my center line, to quote Keith. My only option was to be myself.

Mahalie, Bill's lovely wife, of future friendship to come, was at the center of this. She found the conversational thread that Keith had tossed to her that we were engaged. Which led into a whole dialogue about how no one knew he was yet divorced, since everyone had not been in close contact over the miles and years that had become between all of them. This conversation then transitioned to the next natural thought: "Well now Err-uh-kuh we must see that ring."

With that I realized I couldn't get the long white glove off of my hand and in fact it was stuck on that beautiful oval stone. So to hilarious effect, with the help of Mahalie and perhaps a few of her friends, maybe even with the help of my teeth, we finally hauled off the pesky glove, and finally exposed the beautiful token of Keith's affection.

The one thing Southern women can do better than anyone else in the world, is emote warmth and affection. Perhaps the ladies don't always mean it from the bottom of their hearts. But compared to the

"blue-bellied devils" (to quote my favorite rocker
Tom Petty) from the cold hearted North of my
childhood who could look right through you with
their stony eyes, these Southern Belles were downright
engaging. They turned social obligation into
something moving towards enlightenment.

So after we got through the congratulations on
engagement, the women settled into this Southern-
styled "Who's your Daddy?" discussion.

This amazed me, as we lilted down the fascinating
twists and turns of their convoluted Ancestry.com
discussion before there was such a technology thing.
When the courteous question was thrown my way
asking about my Momma and Daddy, I hesitated for a
moment.

 Now, my eight great-grandparents all came here
separately, long after the Civil War was finished.
Ironically, many of them were miners, so maybe that is
why I felt so at home underground in the granite rock
spa? Anyways, they all came in the Great Migration
when our country figured out we had killed off all the
available masculine labor during the War of Northern
Aggression. There was no one left to mine the coal
that kept us warm in hearth and home.

So with a look of chagrin, I asked, "Mah Daddy?"
with my hand to my heart. I continued in my pretend

Southern draw, "Well, I know this, mah Daddy was a damn Yankee!"

And with that we all laughed, and I commented on how heartwarming it was to hear about all this connection. I found it utterly disarming, especially literally, once I escaped those cloying elbow-length gloves.

~ Discard the kid Gloves
and have Fun being Yourself ~

MEETING THE FAMILY

~ Sometimes we have to Throw the first Stone
at our Own Glass House ~

I would talk on the phone long distance with my family about my relationship with Keith. But it didn't feel right telling them over the phone about our engagement. They had been a wonderful emotional support system for me as I had completed two huge transitions in my life between my divorce and career transfer to Atlanta. Actually surprisingly so. Living in the glass house of a minister's family is never easy. I wasn't sure how excited everyone would be about me charging into a new love chapter in my life, no matter how natural it felt to me. Really, how much change could I inflict on them without them breaking rank at some point?

I spent many hours talking through these unknown variables with Dr. Larry, my counselor. Ironically, Dr. Larry was a Methodist minister just like my Pop, but Larry spent his career as a family counselor, a very different course.

Larry had a knack for helping women like myself express our own voices. This was in stark contrast to others in the church world who were more interested in suppression. Over time, I found that this specialization came from Larry's own life experience.

When I asked a few probing questions, Larry explained how he too struggled with expression when he was a young man. In fact, he had developed a stammer, subsequent to the loss of his own father. As the oldest son he moved into a caretaking role in his own remaining family. From my perspective, it appeared that Larry had turned his personal weakness into the strength of his practice, for he could speak directly to my struggle. If Larry could overcome the insurmountable odds of a stammer, I could find my voice too.

Through these weekly dialogues with Larry, I finally found a place, where I had to choose for me. It was time to stop making decisions for others' approvals. I knew deep in my soul that I had come home, when I looked into Keith's eyes.

We were approaching an Easter weekend and Keith and I were planning a trip up North to visit with our families. It just felt right to tell them in person. This was not going to be an apology tour. It was going to be a coming out party, even if it meant there were only two celebrants.

When I called Pop, the family social calendar, to firm up the Easter weekend plans, I hinted that Keith and I were getting pretty serious and that elementary school age children didn't seem to be slowing Keith down.

Using his Welsh pitch-accent acquired from his Mother, Pop would crow phrases going from a low to a high pitch like "Say it isn't sooooo", which seems to be part of the Welsh "Land of Song" tradition, but who knows. The avid sportsman that he was, he often spoke in athletic colloquialisms too. So after hearing my relationship commentary, Pop belted out, "Well it sounds like Keith is putting on the full court press!" while he laughed and laughed at his own joke.

Well, perhaps, this was going to be a bit easier transition than I thought. But I was still worried more about my Mom. She was very supportive about my decision to divorce my first husband. She had flown to Atlanta a number of times to help the girls transition their young lives. But I wasn't so sure how she would feel about a new marital start. After all, not only was she a minister's wife, but she was also born a minister's daughter. We both knew that minister's daughters were not afforded the same forgiveness and acceptance preached from the pulpit for others. We were held to an entirely different standard, well at least in our own minds. (This point is exactly why I began to joke that I was the rebel in my family because I ran off and became a tax accountant. There were less responsibilities!)

So, on the morning we were to meet my family at my sister Leah's house, I got cold feet. I couldn't predict how my Mom in particular was going to respond to our engagement announcement, and I was afraid that any surprise reaction might really hurt my Brave Heart's feelings. He was a little anxious about my family's acceptance about our age difference. In response, I attempted to explain that physical differences such as age, race, physical incapacity etc. never mattered to my family. The only requirement was if you loved Jesus and practiced your faith every day.

The look on Keith's face was quite skeptical. He asked, "Isn't your father going to care that I can provide for you and your two daughters? He won't have to worry about you anymore."

It was difficult to explain how my Dad, who loved me very much, had never been concerned about my physical well-being. In his mind, it was up to God to provide all of our physical needs. I don't think it had ever occurred to Pop to waste time worrying. He would often quote, "Whether we live or whether we die we are the Lord's." If you live by that mantra on a daily basis, physicality is definitely relegated to the bench.

For example, the first time I brought up the question of how we could afford college costs when I didn't have any small change to pay the turnpike tolls, Pop's response was "God will provide." It was then, I took matters into my own hands, and did my own college financial planning. As many family legacies are complex like mine, I was lost on how to explain to Keith the intricacies of my family's belief system.

So a few hours before our big reveal, I called my Mother. After a few niceties I said, "Mom. I have to tell you something important. When we see you today, we have some big news. Keith and I got engaged, and I wanted to tell you all in person." After her expressions of surprise, I continued, "But at the same time, I just want you to be relaxed. Keith gave me this beautiful engagement ring, and I don't want you to be shocked. It is bigger than our family is used to. And I wanted to give you a heads up before you saw it." I still felt like another shoe was going to drop, maybe it would have been better not to tell Mom. Perhaps it would be better for her to be speechless.

 It was the normal chaotic modge podge of a Swenson holiday dinner. My nephews were crashing through the house. My daughters were with their Dad for the holiday. My sister walked in with her arms full of grocery bags with some last minute food items. Nana, my nonagenarian Grandmother, was even in attendance. Pop and Keith just returned from a walk along the Delaware River, where Keith officially asked for my hand in marriage. Which was hilarious in itself, as the two men were within a year of each other in age. Secretly, I wish I had been a fly along the sidewalk, to see the executive asking for permission of any sort from one of his peers.

Upon their return, in the role of family patriarch, Pop crowed our announcement to the familial crowd, "Well that's it! Now you just gotta set the date for the big day!"

My sister just catching up yelled, "What?! You didn't tell me! You got engaged?" Her face was plastered with a smile ear to ear, I already knew how much she and Keith liked each other. I felt like a CIA operative. By keeping Leah in the dark, I provided her with plausible deniability, in case she was interrogated by friends or family before we were ready to go public. It's funny, as the oldest child, I still tried to protect my siblings.

But our Mom, was already standing next to me. She pivoted to where I was sitting on the couch, and straddled my legs with her own. With a mischievous grin, my Mom questioned, "Now let me see this ring!" Oh no, I had no idea where this was going to go. I held my breath in expectant terror.

After examining my left hand held in her own, my Mom turned to Keith. When confronted with conundrums my Mom often tried to use humor to turn the tables. Sometimes humorous, sometimes not. Upon writing this now I know where I picked up this trait.

Looking Keith, the powerhouse CEO dead in the eye, my Mother, the minister's wife, asked, "Where did you get this? Out of a bubble gum machine?"

~ Just when you think you can Control the Narrative, Guess again ~

CHASING BUBBLE GUM MACHINES

~ Figure out how to use Humor to communicate
your most difficult Emotional Responses,
so you can Enjoy Your own Journey ~

Everything seemed suddenly frozen in time. Keith and I were both speechless. What do you say to that? My preparatory comments seemed to have created more mayhem rather than less. Later that evening after we left the event, we were processing my Mom's bubble gum machine comment. We decided that we were going to use humor as our response. Specifically, Keith said, "Ahmm gonna make it mah mission, come hell or high water, to find that bubble gum machine. Then ahm gonna stock it with those plastic bubble dispensers full of rings! Then Ahmm gonna give it to her as a gift!"

Eventually we did pull off this witty rejoinder. After all, turn-about is fair play. If I fast forwarded to what happened one year later, through a fortuitous round of events, we found a shocked wholesale purveyor who sold us a one-off machine for our own personal prank. He seemed as mystified from my explanation

as Keith was from my Mother's original comment.
After my Mom unwrapped her surprise gift, she was
having difficulty connecting the dots. Until I
reminded her of her now infamous quote. At that
point she fell off her chair, laughing and laughing.
Being the good sport she was, she took the bubble
gum machine home with her and forever thereafter
dispensed plastic toy rings for her grandchildren each
time they came to visit.

~ *Be sure you want to Know the Answer*
Before asking a Question ~

THE FEMALE CARAVAN

~ The Answer often resides in Symbolic Markers
along the Way of our Journey ~

After much angst, we decided in the long run it would be better to start our new combined life in Florida at Keith's home. He had a more established life there than I had after my move for a career relocation. On other factual matters, there was no winter in South Florida and the infamous Atlanta traffic would become a distant memory.

Now, you would think it would be quite easy to just jump in the car and ride on down to Palm Beach, also known as the Beverly Hills of the East Coast. But when you think on mid-career single Moms living alone with two young daughters, you know simplicity is a quantum leap. The devil lives in the details of the logistics.

When I began to chart our transition, I had another heartfelt discussion with Keith. We were trying to do so much in a tight timeframe, primarily so the girls could start at their new Palm Beach school in September. We wanted to smooth out as many bumps as possible in another new chapter in their young lives. Therefore I laid out our logistical battle plan. I wanted to handle my Atlanta move, while Keith cleared the field at his home in Florida. He had closets to empty, furniture to rearrange. He was transforming his lovely home prepared for a golfing retirement into a haven for three new family members, two of which were elementary aged step-daughters.

We had a schedule to meet, and that was something I knew how to do!! We had a wedding to fit into our timeframe as well. And we weren't going to miss that come hell or highwater! Road trips and furniture re-configurations were necessary but seemed trivial. It was like a tax deadline, if we worked in tandem in coordinated effort across state lines, we could "get 'er done" as the comedian Larry the Cable Guy would say.

There were cats to move, a heartfelt request for Lizzie the super nanny to consider relocation with us, there were new private schools to apply to. Endless nights of sifting through personal possessions for the keep, give away and trash piles. As you would expect, it was also difficult to work this move out with the girls' father. There were anxious discussions with Dr. Larry, a child therapist, for Hannah and Chloe.

During the fury of packing, Hannah reminded me, "Mommy, I need to be occupied." Everyone needs to have jobs, it gives us purpose and therefore defines our value. So we set up two cardboard moving boxes on the back porch for Hannah and Chloe to paint and decorate their "cat boxes". These would be the sanctuary houses for the cats, Lucky Miranda and Samantha to feel "safe" during our arduous journey in the minivan.

 But the boxes served another purpose, it provided a creative outlet for each daughter during the anxious time of packing. Also, it provided an object completely in their control. Lastly, they were creating with their own hands sanctuary for their respective charges. Those sanctuary boxes remained until each daughter was ready to throw them out, for they became symbolic markers of our journeys.

So, finally, one steamy day in August the female caravan hit I-75 South for Palm Beach, Florida. Leah, my deeply supportive sister, had flown in to help me pack the house. After pulling a few strings, she adjusted her own schedule so she could remain and help me drive South to move into Keith's home.

 Ensconced in the middle row captain's chairs, Hannah and Chloe could enjoy the new fangled concept of TV screens installed in the back of the first row's headrests. Suddenly, kids had their own movie theater. As Hannah sorted through the CDs and they settled on The Lion King. The full circle of life, how applicable. The negotiation was Hannah got to pick the movie, while Chloe got to pick the formatting, wide screen or full screen. When asked Chloe would lisp every time, "Full Scream", which we found so adorable.

And yes we were definitely in Full Scream mode ourselves, as we hurtled down the road. The back of the minivan was reserved for the cats in their cardboard city. As this was their first road trip, they were in feline full scream for hours on end with motion sickness.

And most importantly, tailing right behind us was Lizzie in her Honda. After much consternation, she decided to make the journey with us. Worst case, she could always return. But having her move with us, brought a sense of peaceful continuity. All would be right with the world, with our own Mary Poppins joining the new adventure.

We drove through the mind bending thunderous electric storms in the belly of Central Florida's plains. We drove through sheets of rain going 15 m.p.h. down the Florida Turnpike in the pitch dark, bumper to bumper with other nearly invisible automobiles creeping along in their own miserable circles of flashing hazards.

This was when it was still legal to use your hazards, now it could hazard a warrant for one's arrest, which has never really been explained to me. I understand the obvious hazards of texting, but the actual hazards are hazardous? Thank God we have so many regulators to regulate safety back into our lives, otherwise where would we all be? I couldn't hazard a guess.

 After the hundredth flash of lightning, I suddenly quaked. Was this some kind of sign? Were the heavens opening up this deluge just for me? Was this some kind of biblical judgment? I had never seen anything like this. When it finally lightened up, my knuckles were still white and so stiff from gripping the steering wheel for dear life.

By the time we finally arrived that night it was about 1 a.m. Even at that time, Keith still looked quite dapper in a golf shirt, neatly trimmed belt, khakis and loafers. As Keith barged out the front door of Tradewind Drive, he saw little girls, cats, and Barbies spilling from the mini-van, followed by three exhausted women stumbling out of the two cars.

His masculine in-charge personality, must have taken a shock to his system, because he bellowed out in that deep voice, "I am surrounded by a sea of estrogen!"

He kissed me in relief heralding our safe arrival, I quipped, "Yes it took all of us girls to level the playing field." And I meant it, Keith was a gale force wind all by himself.

~ Merges come in many Shapes and Sizes ~

LEARNING TO FLY

~ Pink Floyd sang this Truth, but sometimes we must first Grow a New kind of Wings ~

We sorted out the bedroom wars and other more minor sisterly pecking orders, where everything had to be exactly even and equal. We assembled the beginnings of our new found domestic peace. We found the school uniform store and Lizzie's temporary apartment.

Then my mind returned to my job. My hard earned ticket to freedom of some sorts. By choosing Keith, it subsequently became a choice between marriage and my current employer. Why you may ask? Just as I valued my own independent career, the Public Accounting Industry was built on Independence rules too. We provided objective, independent opinions on public companies' financial statements. If my firm didn't appear independent from influence on these opinions, their value was gone and so was the firm. One firm had already gone up in smoke over this issue, so it was a very tender subject.

Also, after Keith retired, he still served as an outside director for a number of public companies that my

firm audited. From the public's view, how
independent would my firm's Opinions look if it was
known that Keith's wife was a partner at the same
firm?

It could have the appearance of undue influence.
Even though I had actually no influence over what an
audit partner rendered as an Opinion, it was still a
problem of optics.

As we started our journey towards marital bliss, I gave
my notice to my firm. A transfer to the local office
was not a viable option. But I wasn't sure if I was
quite ready to quit my career altogether. Not only had
I spent years working, but years in training. It seemed
to render it all completely pointless if I didn't keep up
at some level.

I explored some other career options, and obtained
job offers from two banks in Palm Beach. But I was
still afraid. Trust had been a long time coming, and I
was still working on my cerebral blind spot. After all,
when did I last trust pretty much anyone? What if I
made all these changes and Keith regretted our newly
forged partnership? What if he loathed paying for my
children's future education?

It was unnerving. I knew my center-line of security
was over work. So, I didn't really trust myself to go
jump into a high pressure career setting, I would be
right back at outworking everybody else, late nights.

Yet, here I was starting this new life with my soul mate. I could see my two daughters in daylight and make lunches and drop them off at school. Why did I feel the need to rush off into a corporate office away from my new found domestic bliss?

After years of fear and distrust, it was going to take some time to unwind these emotions, and it wasn't going to happen over night. I still craved working. So it felt good to have job offers in my hip pocket. It took me a bit to work through that I didn't really want the new job. I just needed it as my own sanctuary box just like the cats and my daughters did.

 In the regulatory forest of accounting code enforcement, there is a technical definition called "close participation." Laughing to myself, I knew that Keith and I were redefining this term in a more romantic way. And new definitions aren't always a comfortable thing. Yes we were jumping off a cliff, but isn't that the only way one can learn how to fly?

 I was a work-horse yes. But I had found a peaceful pasture with Keith. Did I really need to keep this breakneck gallop going forever? It was time for respite.

~ Keep working towards a New Solution,
you may Surprise Yourself ~

ROCKING LIKE A HURRICANE

~ Sometimes Fast and Furious is best.
Rip the Band-Aid right Off ~

After a whirlwind of two weeks, we were settled and we were finally ready to celebrate our Day One. Since our lives had so many moving parts, it wasn't easy to determine our actual wedding date. While we were figuring it out, we referred to it as our Day One. It was our secret code and then mantra as we tiptoed through the field of familial anxieties as we searched for a date of mutual convenience for all, which of course doesn't really exist. As a reminder of the many mine fields that we had traveled together hand in hand on our journey to our new life partnership, I asked the jeweler to engrave "Day One" on the inside of Keith's wedding band.

We chose to marry before the girls' started at their new school in Palm Beach. Therefore we were right at the end of August, as classes began the day after Labor Day, old school style. We wanted the four of us to start off with defined clarity as an official family grouping.

Like many people today our closest friends and family lived around the globe. Both of our lives had been in physical transition for the last couple of years, so our circles of daily friends were changing. We wanted something intimate and private, we both had had the big wedding hooplas the first time around. And both of those marriages ended with a whole lot of hoopla too. We were ready for serenity.

I think I would have been happy at the Town Hall, but Keith had some other ideas. Throughout his professional life, golf and its sacred grounds around the world featured prominently as the place where Keith forged relationships of trust with his peers. If your company is taking huge risks and trying to decide to buy or sell billion dollar acquisitions, to quote Keith, you kinda "want to see the whites of their eyes" before signing your name in blood and letting the rest of the world judge your business acumen via your stock price.

Through the years, Keith had golfed at many courses around the world. And if you had the opportunity to read his personal life story, you would see this list of courses where he had belonged or played over the years. At night when other people counted sheep, Keith played from memory, golf holes from courses he had played throughout his life until he slept. After all he was a Scotsman, from the isles where the cruel sport was invented, it was in his blood.

He wanted to host our closest friends and family at one of his favorite venues in the world, Laurel Valley Golf Club, where he and a number of other industrial executives belonged over the years. For those of you who avoid the tortured game on the links, you probably don't recognize this club's name. But you probably know the name of Arnold Palmer. Yes, Arnold was an actual real person, not just that refreshing elixir of iced tea and lemonade in a can that was named after him.

Arnold was one of six founding members of this gorgeous place in Ligonier, Pennsylvania, because it was down the road from where he was born and raised. The club was named for the Mountain Laurel that grows on the rolling hills of Western Pennsylvania.

Today, if you visit the 9-11 Memorial to United Flight 93 in Shanksville, you are only about a twenty minute drive from Laurel Valley. In fact on that September Eleventh, the caddies on the course saw the troubled plane flying extremely low as it began its final descent.

As required, Keith asked permission from the club's president to have our wedding on their golfing hallowed grounds. And we found that we were the first wedding to ever be hosted at this special place. This magical place, had a row of red brick romantic cottages along a sweeping ridge that crowned the sparkling green fairways. It was just the right accomodations for our close crowd for friends and family to house, in this semi-rural location.

About forty family and friends flew in from around the world to join us for the weekend. My brother, who lived in China at the time, surprised us and flew for two days straight so he could attend. Family and friends traveled from Florida, South Carolina, California and the greater Northeast. From Atlanta, Dr. Larry came with his wife, so he could marry us. His timely, pertinent support made it a double blessing to have him perform the service.

Keith's friend from his youth, Bill Davies, the very same that I met on our engagement, and his wife Mahalie, flew in too. In fact, out of all of us gathered together, it was Mahalie that had the surprise benefit of meeting Mr. Arnold Palmer, one of the Fathers of golf that fair day. He wandered into his club to see what all the hub-bub was about. And true to his nature, he stopped and signed some golf balls for Mahalie's grandchildren. What a special treat, always the gentleman and ambassador of his sport.

Terence, Keith's best friend in business, and his wife joined us from South Africa. This is the same Terence, that I wrote about in Love & Taxes, Book One. Together the two men worked as an alliance on their joint venture so both companies would benefit and couldn't harm the other, Terence's mining company and Keith's employer as their largest buyer.

By trusting and working with each other they changed the world for the better. There was now enough platinum group metals to build the newly invented catalytic converters, which made cleaner exhaust systems on every car, until they combined forces and built a new supply chain.

On a personal level, it felt like Keith and I were doing something of the same. We were reinventing ourselves, trusting each other as we remodeled our own lives. It wasn't easy, but we found our own way, and we were ready to celebrate.

Now we, the joyous wedding couple, had to get from Palm Beach, Florida where we just set up house, to Laurel Valley to seal our own nuptials. No problem, we'd just jump on a plane right?

Wrong!

Hurricane Katrina had something else in mind. She was planning her first assault on America in Southern Florida before she continued her crawl. Within a few days of our wedding, it became clear that our own flight out was under threat of cancellation due to the early gale force winds' impact on commercial flights. As millions of Floridian residents scrambled to get out of her way, we didn't have earlier flight options. Were we going to have to drive a few thousand miles in forty-eight hours with two little girls to make our own wedding? That sounded daunting, and par for our course.

What was it with these hurricanes and gale force winds? There was definitely symbolism here, as the winds of change swept through our own lives. But nothing was going to slow us down, not even this force of nature. This was one more test, it was just one of a more physical kind. Nothing was going to hold us back from our destiny to walk down that aisle. We were going to get there come hell or high water, literally.

As we were becoming pragmatic experts in logistics, Keith made an executive-level decision and chartered a small jet. That sounded scary to me too. I knew three different women throughout my life, all of which lost their pilot-fathers in small plane crashes, along with other family members. It was a risk I didn't like taking. I preferred not to see my pilots, and let them remain anonymous in the cockpit of a gigantic Boeing 747. But desperate times call for desperate measures.

As Katrina barreled down on Palm Beach International Airport, we boarded the jet, the first time any of us girls had had this surreal experience. We settled into our seats. I was on my Blackberry ready to cancel our commercial tickets, when suddenly the engine died and it wasn't coming back on! The charter flight was un-chartered. We were in uncharted territory again! We had thirty minutes to make our original commercial flight, over in another terminal. There was still a shot that Delta made the tarmac and took off, before the bosses shut down the airport due to swirling high winds.

What was happening! We were going to have to carry on, because we had missed the cut off for checking any luggage, we had to run straight for the gate!

The one thing I had to find in my suitcase was my wedding dress! That beautiful, sleek, creamy rose pink evening gown that was my own take on a new start. Thank God it was a wrinkle free synthetic material! I rolled it up around my right forearm, and jammed it into my carryon. I found one pair of heels, not the right ones, and stuffed them in their too.

Chloe was too small to keep up with our adult legs charging for the gate. I slung her up on my right hip, threw my bag over my left shoulder and took off. I could hear Keith's voice reverberating through the airport behind me as he pulled all the carry ons and kept Hannah close. I was going to stand in the doorway of the airplane if need be, until we were all safely on board!

Somehow, someway, we made it. Our plane was one of the last to take off that day before the airport closed for Hurricane Katrina's arrival. Through darkening skies, we ascended. As we breached the cloud cover, our cabin exploded with radiant sunlight.

Dust motes danced in the air like tiny glistening diamonds. One sunbeam shot through my engagement ring, spangling a rainbow spectrum of tiny spinning prisms across every surface in the row of our seats.

The sudden contrast of darkness and light was a visceral reminder to me. When we pursue a dream, we often are fumbling in the dark as we strive to turn it into a reality. It is often a soggy march through swamps before breaking out into the sunlight of triumph. After marching with our heads down to ensure we don't slip and stumble, our final achievement can be almost blindingly fleeting.

~As the Theologian penned
long before the Crooners' sang,
"The Darkest hour is just before Dawn" ~

THE TERRACE

~ When you wrestle the winds of Fate, Pause to joyfully Celebrate your hard won Achievements ~

Our small tribe of guests were gathered and seated, outside on the Terrace of the Palmer Pavilion. Despite gale force winds trying to subvert our marital flight plans, we were all assembled. Hannah and Chloe were intent on their flower girl tasks, they were dropping rose petals all along the way in their sequined pastel pink dresses. When dressing for the occasion, I committed a small faux pas that could have been an emotional disaster for my eldest. Mistakenly, I had cut Hannah's sandal strap as I removed the store tags. Thankfully, with a few safety pins in place, Hannah could perform her flower girl duties foregoing the embarrassment of bare feet.

I selected my dark pink dress by Nicole Miller, for a few reasons. Besides pink being my favorite color, I loved the designer's signature knack for draping versatile fabric. But there was something else. Laurel Valley's unique member's blazer was light pink in ode to the mountain flower. Men were required to wear it to dinner when on the premises, if they were

members. I wanted my dress to compliment Keith's
jacket, so it was clear that we were a solid pair. Yes we
were different yet synchronized. And I loved that we
sizzled in pink. It was a unique clothing statement,
just as we were a one-of-a-kind couple.

As Dr. Larry read the vows that he wrote especially for
us, we looked West over the terrace on the rolling hills
of Western Pennsylvania. The eighteenth green
shown like an emerald. The massive pine trees
marched down the sloping fairway and surrounded the
green like staunch guardians, where they met the slate
blue grays of the lake slicing through the fairway.
Overcast skies reminded me of Carrara marble carved
by the hand of Michelangelo himself.

As he finished with his benediction, Mother Nature
decided to sprinkle us with her own silvery blessing of
a misting rain. Just a gentle reminder that she was
with us too.

Off in the future there were unforeseen adventures
and travails. But for that moment, time stood still and
held its breath as we raised our faces to the skies in
grateful, soulful delight.

*~ Let the Future carry its own Burdens,
and just Enjoy today's Moments ~*

❧

ACKNOWLEDGEMENTS

Dearest Hannah and Chloe,

You two are the ultimate insiders as you lived this book along with us. Often living the story is a lot more granular than is clear in its retelling. You both accomplished this with faith and grace. Please know that we are spellbound by what you are each building in your own story books. We watch in awe as you move forward, framing your own future outcomes.

All my love, Mom

Dearest Keith,

I know over the years, there have been countless times where I expressed my regret for finding you "so late". But also remember that I promised you this: the next time around, I will come find you again, and it won't take me so long. For then I will recognize your broad Scottish back anywhere, and thank God you don't know how to whisper. For I will follow the sound of your voice that still makes the hairs in my ear canals stand tall. And you will recall our secret code words when I whisper them into your ear one more time: DAY ONE.

All my love, EE

❦

RECOMMENDED
READING LIST

Leaders on Leading: Insights from the Field

Time, Real and Imaginary, an Allegory by Samuel T. Coleridge

Journey of Souls, Dr. Brian Weiss

Opus Vino: An Encyclopedia on Wine

The Unexpected Legacy of Divorce: A Twenty-Five Year Landmark Study, Dr. Judith Wallerstein

Powers of Two: How Relationships Drive Creativity, Joshua Wolf Shenk

Art & Fear: Observations on the Perils (and Rewards) of Artmaking, David Bayles and Ted Orland

The Secret History of the World as Laid Down by the Secret Societies, Mark Booth

❧⨳❧

WORK WITH ME

There are a number of ways that you can work with me: an introductory entrepreneurial program, ongoing support and individual business development management.

You can sign up for a special advisory intensive offering where you can work with me one-on-one at **ericaswensonelliott.com**. Here is where you can also find my various books and artistic endeavors.

I am also the proud co-founder of **bizbooks.expert**, where we offer boutique tax, bookkeeping and custom advisory services to select clients.

I have a soft spot for all courageous entrepreneurs out there and am thrilled to help them spread their wings into the world of independent prosperity and success. For start-ups and small ventures, I created Endeavor University, an educational subscription service of video tutorials. This tool can get you started on a prudent budget with immediate access. Find it at **endeavoruniversity.com**.

For all other inquiries about my various books and artistic endeavors, you can always reach out to me at **ericaswensonelliott.com**.

LOVE & BUSINESS by Erica S. Elliott

ABOUT THE AUTHOR

Erica Elliott has an unusual set of gifts. As a prominent tax accountant and also an author and artist at heart, she finds great joy in creating order from chaos and inspiration through her writing. Where other people get dizzy with numbers, she sees clarity and creates profitable, practical magic. The author was brought up in a quite unorthodox yet loving household: friendly with Healers and finding purpose through communal connection. This upbringing allowed her to see people, circumstances and things in unusual ways. Her early memories were first falling in love with numbers, words, and then drawing, all symbols pointing us along the mystical journey of life. She encourages everyone to follow and recognize all of their unique, diverse gifts, no matter how many they carry. Yes, you can be an accountant, artist and author!

Visit the author online at **ericaswensonelliott.com.**

೪ೲ

www.ingramcontent.com/pod-product-compliance
Lightning Source LLC
Chambersburg PA
CBHW060527210326
41519CB00014B/3145